Focus in High School Mathematics

Focus in High School Mathematics

Reasoning and Sense Making

NATIONAL COUNCIL OF
TEACHERS OF MATHEMATICS

Copyright © 2009 by
THE NATIONAL COUNCIL OF TEACHERS OF MATHEMATICS, INC.
1906 Association Drive, Reston, VA 20191-1502
(703) 620-9840; (800) 235-7566; www.nctm.org
All rights reserved
Fourth printing 2011

Library of Congress Cataloging-in-Publication Data

Focus in high school mathematics : reasoning and sense making.
    p. cm.
  Includes bibliographical references.
  ISBN 978-0-87353-631-8
  1. Mathematics—Study and teaching (Secondary)—United States.
  2. Curriculum planning—United States. I. National Council of Teachers of Mathematics.
  QA13.F63 2009
  510.71'273—dc22
                        2009032015

The National Council of Teachers of Mathematics is a public voice
of mathematics education, supporting teachers to ensure equitable
mathematics learning of the highest quality for all students through vision,
leadership, professional development, and research.

Focus in High School Mathematics: Reasoning and Sense Making
is an official position of the National Council of Teachers of Mathematics
as approved by its Board of Directors, April 2009.

Printed in the United States of America

Contents

List of Examples

National Council of Teachers of Mathematics High School Curriculum Project

Writing Group

W. Gary Martin, *Chair*
Professor of Mathematics Education
Auburn University

John A. Carter, *NCTM Board Liaison*
Assistant Principal for Teaching and Learning
Adlai E. Stevenson (Illinois) High School

Susan Forster
Mathematics Department Chair and Teacher
Bismarck (North Dakota) High School

Roger Howe
Professor of Mathematics
Yale University

Gary D. Kader
Professor of Mathematical Sciences
Appalachian State University

Henry (Hank) Kepner
President, National Council of Teachers of Mathematics
Professor, Mathematics Education
University of Wisconsin—Milwaukee

Judith Reed Quander, *Staff Liaison*
Director of Research
National Council of Teachers of Mathematics

William McCallum
Professor of Mathematics
University of Arizona

Eric Robinson
Professor of Mathematics
Ithaca College

Vincent Snipes
Professor of Mathematics Education
Director, Center for Mathematics, Science, and
  Technology Education
Winston-Salem State University

Patricia Valdez
Mathematics Department Chair and Teacher
Pájaro Valley (California) High School

Planning Group

W. Gary Martin, *Chair*
Professor of Mathematics Education
Auburn University

Ruth Casey, *NCTM Board Liaison*
  (2007–2008)
PIMSER
University of Kentucky

Fred L. Dillon, *NCTM Board Liaison*
  (2008–2009)
Mathematics Teacher
Strongsville (Ohio) High School

Kaye Forgione
Senior Associate, Mathematics
Achieve, Inc.

Ken Krehbiel, *Staff Liaison*
Associate Executive Director for
Communications
NCTM

Judith Reed Quander, *Staff Liaison*
Director of Research
NCTM

Henry Kepner
President, National Council of Teachers
  of Mathematics
Professor, Mathematics Education
University of Wisconsin—Milwaukee

Jennifer J. Salls, *NCTM Board Liaison*
  (2008–2009)
Mathematics Teacher
Sparks (Nevada) High School

Richard Schaar
Texas Instruments

9-12 Curriculum Task Force

Ruth Casey, *Chair and Board Liaison*
PIMSER
University of Kentucky

Martha Aliaga
Director of Education
American Statistical Association

Hyman Bass
Professor of Mathematics
University of Michigan

John A. Carter, NCTM Board Liaison
Assistant Principal for Teaching and Learning
Adlai E. Stevenson (Illinois) High School

Kaye Forgione
Senior Associate, Mathematics
Achieve, Inc.

Albert Goetz, *Staff Liaison*
Senior Mathematics Editor
NCTM

W. Gary Martin
Professor of Mathematics Education
Auburn University

William McCallum
Professor of Mathematics
University of Arizona

Zalman Usiskin
Professor of Education
University of Chicago

Preface

Background

The National Council of Teachers of Mathematics (NCTM) has a long tradition of providing leadership and vision to support teachers in ensuring equitable mathematics learning of the highest quality for all students. In the three decades since the 1980 publication of *An Agenda for Action,* NCTM has consistently advocated a coherent prekindergarten through grade 12 mathematics curriculum focused on mathematical problem solving. NCTM refined this message in *Curriculum and Evaluation Standards for School Mathematics* (1989), which argued for a common core of mathematics for all students, with attention to the processes of problem solving, reasoning, connections, and communication. Continuing to provide leadership in 2000, NCTM issued *Principles and Standards for School Mathematics* (*Principles and Standards*) (2000a), which updated and elaborated on the 1989 recommendations in a set of five Content Standards and five Process Standards to include in every school mathematics program. In 2006, the Council's *Curriculum Focal Points for Prekindergarten through Grade 8 Mathematics* (*Curriculum Focal Points*) (NCTM 2006a) offered guidance on how to focus the mathematical content for each grade level from prekindergarten through grade 8 while reminding educators of the importance of consistently embedding the relevant mathematical processes throughout the content in every mathematical learning experience.

Realizing a parallel need for focus and coherence at the high school level, although perhaps of a different kind from that addressed in *Curriculum Focal Points* (NCTM 2006a), a 2006 NCTM task force recommended the development of a framework based on *Principles and Standards* (NCTM 2000a) that would guide future work regarding high school mathematics. As a result, a writing group was appointed to produce the framework outlined in this publication. Concurrently, a planning committee was appointed to oversee the larger high school curriculum project, which included guiding the review process for this publication; planning its rollout, including pamphlets summarizing the vision presented in this publication for various audiences; and proposing a series of topic books that elaborate the publication's core messages.

Purpose

This publication advocates that all high school mathematics programs focus on reasoning and sense making. The audience for this publication is intended to be everyone involved in decisions regarding high school mathematics programs, including formal decision makers within the system; people charged with implementing those decisions; and other stakeholders affected by, and involved in, those decisions.

A number of publications produced over the past few years have provided detailed analyses of the topics that should be addressed in each course of high school mathematics (cf. American Diploma Project 2004; College Board 2006, 2007; ACT 2007; Achieve 2007a, 2007b.) This publication takes a somewhat different approach, proposing curricular emphases and instructional approaches that make reasoning and sense making foundational to the content that is taught and learned. Along with the more-detailed content recommendations outlined in *Principles and Standards,* this publication supplies a critical filter in examining any curriculum arrangement to ensure that the ultimate goals of the high school mathematics program are achieved.

Organization of the Publication

The first section of the publication presents an overview of reasoning and sense making. Chapter 1 describes what constitutes reasoning and sense making in the mathematics classroom; why they should be considered as foundational for high school mathematics; and how they link with other mathematical processes, such as representation, communication, connections, and problem solving. Chapter 2 describes in more detail the mathematical reasoning habits that students should continue to acquire throughout their high school mathematics experiences, a general trajectory for how they develop, suggestions for how to promote them in the classroom, and an explanation of how reasoning and sense making fit into the larger picture of mathematical activity.

The second section of the publication demonstrates with examples how reasoning and sense making can be incorporated into the high school curriculum. Chapter 3 provides an overview, and chapters 4–8 describe how reasoning and sense making fit into five overarching areas of high school mathematics—number and measurement, algebraic symbols, functions, geometry, and statistics and probability.

The final section discusses issues in implementing reasoning and sense making across the high school mathematics program. Chapter 9 focuses on how to provide equitable opportunities for all students to engage in reasoning and sense making. Chapter 10 addresses the importance of coherent expectations regarding curriculum, instruction, and assessment in promoting reasoning and sense making. Finally, chapter 11 presents questions to consider as stakeholders work together to improve high school mathematics education.

For the convenience of the reader, an annotated bibliography is included that describes pertinent research works that underlie this publication, organized by chapter.

Acknowledgments

Focus in High School Mathematics: Reasoning and Sense Making reflects more than two years of effort by a large group of mathematicians, mathematics educators, curriculum developers, policymakers, and classroom practitioners. In addition to those playing a formal role in developing the publication and the broader high school curriculum project, many dedicated persons provided formal reviews at various stages in the publication's preparation. Without their candid and constructive input, this publication would not have been possible. The Board of Directors and writing group extend sincere thanks to the following individuals:

Dave Barnes
Hyman Bass
Richelle Blair
Jim Bohan
David M. Bressoud
Gail Burrill
Carlos A. Cabana
Al Cuoco
Fred Dillon
John A. Dossey
Joan Ferrini-Mundy
Christine Franklin
Shirley M. Frye
David C. Geary
Karen J. Graham

Eric W. Hart
M. Kathleen Heid
Linda Kaniecki
Tim Kanold
David Kapolka
Mike Koehler
Henry Kranendonk
Jim Lanich
Matt Larson
Steve Leinwand
Jim Lewis
Mary M. Lindquist
Johnny W. Lott
Carol E. Malloy
Sharon McCrone

Claire Pierce
Jack Price
Michael Roach
James M. Rubillo
Alan H. Schoenfeld
Richard L. Scheaffer
Cathy Seeley
J. Michael Shaughnessy
Jenny Salls
Barbara Shreve
Marilyn E. Strutchens
Christine D. Thomas
Nancy Washburn
Stephen S. Willoughby
Estelle Woodbury

NCTM's membership was also invited to provide input on a public draft posted in August 2008. We express our sincere appreciation to all the individuals and groups who submitted their insights and expertise. Their reactions were effectively summarized by the RMC Research Corporation and guided the preparation of the final publication.

We give final thanks to several persons who provided invaluable assistance in the preparation of the publication, including Lauretta Garrett, Stephen Stuckwisch, and Narendra Govil at Auburn University, as well as the NCTM staff who carefully edited and created an effective layout, including Ann Butterfield and Randy White.

From the President

With the interest generated by the publication in 2006 of *Curriculum Focal Points for Prekindergarten through Grade 8 Mathematics: A Quest for Coherence,* we were frequently asked, "When are you going to do something for high school?" In January 2007, the NCTM Board of Directors charged a group of writers with the task of producing a "conceptual framework to guide the development of future publications and tools related to 9–12 mathematics curriculum and instruction." With this publication, I am pleased to present the product of that charge: *Focus in High School Mathematics: Reasoning and Sense Making.*

The writing group decided to address high school mathematics by focusing on students' reasoning and sense making, which are at the core of all mathematical learning and understanding. Reasoning is the process of drawing conclusions based on evidence or stated assumptions—extending the knowledge that one has at a given moment. Sense making is developing understanding of a situation, concept, or context by connecting it with existing knowledge. Reasoning and sense making are at the heart of mathematics from early childhood through adulthood. A high school mathematics curriculum based on reasoning and sense making will prepare students for higher learning, the workplace, and productive citizenship.

On behalf of the Board of Directors, I want to express my deep gratitude to W. Gary Martin for his tireless efforts in leading this project and to thank everyone who made this publication possible. The writers of *Focus in High School Mathematics: Reasoning and Sense Making* include mathematics educators and high school teachers, an administrator, mathematicians, and a statistician. Their contributions will guide the further development and improvement of high school mathematics education for years to come. I also extend sincere thanks to the planning group for their guidance throughout the process and to all those who submitted reviews through the development process for helping to shape this publication.

Henry S. Kepner Jr.
President, National Council of Teachers of Mathematics

Section 1

Defining Reasoning and Sense Making

Chapter 1

Reasoning and Sense Making

A high school mathematics program based on reasoning and sense making will prepare students for citizenship, for the workplace, and for further study.

HIGH school mathematics prepares students for possible postsecondary work and study in three broad areas (cf. NCTM [2000a]):

1. Mathematics for life

2. Mathematics for the workplace

3. Mathematics for the scientific and technical community

As the demands for mathematical literacy increase, students face challenges in all three areas. First, the report of the Programme for International Student Assessment (2007) suggests that students in the United States are lagging in mathematical literacy, which that report defines as the ability to apply mathematics "to analyse, reason and communicate effectively as they pose, solve and interpret mathematical problems in a variety of situations" (p. 304), including as future citizens. Second, globalization and the rise of technology are presenting new economic and workforce challenges (Friedman 2007), and the traditional mathematics curriculum is insufficient for students entering many fields (Ganter and Barker 2004). Finally, the United States is in danger of losing its leadership position in science, technology, engineering, and mathematics (Task Force on the Future of American Innovation 2005; Committee on Science, Engineering and Public Policy 2006; Tapping America's Potential 2008).

A focus on reasoning and sense making, when developed in the context of important content, will ensure that students can accurately carry out mathematical procedures, understand why those procedures work, and know how they might be used and their results interpreted. This understanding will expand students' abilities to apply mathematical perspectives, concepts, and tools flexibly in each of the three areas mentioned above. Such a focus on reasoning and sense making will produce citizens who make informed and reasoned decisions, including quantitatively sophisticated choices about their personal finances, about which public policies deserve their support, and about which insurance or health plans to select. It will also produce workers who can satisfy the increased mathematical needs in professional areas ranging from health care to small business to digital technology (American Diploma Project 2004).

A high school curriculum that focuses on reasoning and sense making will help satisfy the increasing demand for scientists, engineers, and mathematicians while preparing students for whatever professional, vocational, or technical needs may arise. Recent studies suggest that students will experience career changes multiple times during their lives (U.S. Department of Labor 2006), and many of the jobs they will hold in the future do not yet exist. Mathematics is increasingly essential for a wide range of careers, including finance, advertising, forensics, and sports journalism. The advent of the Internet has produced an explosion of new careers in mathematics and statistics that involve harnessing the huge amount of data at people's fingertips (Baker and Leak 2006). By emphasizing both content and reasoning ability, high school mathematics programs can help prepare workers who are able to navigate this uncharted territory.

What Are Reasoning and Sense Making?

In the most general terms, reasoning can be thought of as the process of drawing conclusions on the basis of evidence or stated assumptions. Although reasoning is an important part of all disciplines, it plays a special and fundamental role in mathematics. Reasoning in mathematics is often understood to encompass formal reasoning, or proof, in which conclusions are logically deduced from assumptions and definitions. However, mathematical reasoning can take many forms, ranging from informal explanation and justification to formal deduction, as well as inductive observations. Reasoning often begins with explorations, conjectures at various levels, false starts, and partial explanations before a result is reached. As students develop a repertoire of increasingly sophisticated methods of reasoning and proof during their time in high school, "standards for accepting explanations should become more stringent" (NCTM 2000a, p. 342).

We define sense making as developing understanding of a situation, context, or concept by connecting it with existing knowledge. In practice, reasoning and sense making are intertwined across the continuum from informal observations to formal deductions, as seen in figure 1.1, despite the common perception that identifies sense making with the informal end of the continuum and reasoning, especially proof, with the more formal end.

Fig. 1.1. The relationship of reasoning and sense making

On one hand, formal reasoning may be based on sense making in which one identifies common elements across a number of observations and realizes how those common elements connect with previously experienced situations. On the other hand, "a good proof is one that also helps one understand the meaning of what is being proved: to see not only that it is true but also why it is true" (Yackel and Hanna 2003, p.228). As sense making develops, it increasingly incorporates more formal elements. For instance, in example 8, "Squaring It Away," when asked to solve a quadratic equation, students use an informal geometric model to complete the square of the trinomial but then, realizing that more than one solution may exist, they extend the ideas they have developed with more formal algebra to find both solutions.

Mathematical reasoning and sense making are both important outcomes of mathematics instruction, as well as important means by which students come to know mathematics. As the term is used in this publication, *mathematical reasoning* encompasses statistical reasoning; see "Statistical Reasoning" in chapter 2.

Why Reasoning and Sense Making?

This publication emphasizes that reasoning and sense making are the foundations of the NCTM Process Standards (2000a). The processes of mathematics—Problem Solving, Reasoning and Proof, Connections, Communication, and Representation—are all manifestations of the act of making sense of mathematics and of reasoning as defined above. Problem solving and proof are impossible without reasoning, and both are avenues through which students develop mathematical reasoning and make sense of mathematical ideas. The communications, connections, and representations chosen by a student must support reasoning and sense making, and reasoning must be employed in making those decisions.

Proof is a communication of formal reasoning built on a foundation of sense making, and it is an important outcome of mathematical thinking. Proof can (1) explain why a particular mathematical result must be true, (2) develop autonomous learners by providing the skills needed to evaluate the validity of their own reasoning and that of others, and (3) reveal connections and provide insight into the underlying structure of mathematics (Knuth 2000). Regardless of the specific format of a proof, students may use formal reasoning to make connections with prior learning, extend thinking, support articulation, and stimulate reflection.

At the high school level, reasoning and sense making are of particular importance, but historically "reasoning" has been limited to very select areas of the high school curriculum, and sense making is in many instances not present at all. However, an emphasis on students' reasoning and sense making can help students organize their knowledge in ways that enhance the development of number sense, algebraic fluency, functional relationships, geometric reasoning, and statistical thinking, as exemplified in section 2. When students connect new learning with their existing knowledge, they are more likely to understand and retain the new information (Hiebert 2003) than when it is simply presented as a list of isolated procedures. Without such conceptual understanding, "learning new topics becomes harder since there is no network of previously learned concepts and skills to link a new topic to" (Kilpatrick, Swafford, and Findell 2001, p. 123), meaning that procedures may be forgotten as quickly as they are apparently learned. A refocus on reasoning and sense making will increase understanding and foster meaning.

How Do We Include Reasoning and Sense Making in the Classroom?

Reasoning and sense making should occur in every mathematics classroom every day. In such an environment, teachers and students ask and answer such questions as "What's going on here?" and "Why do you think that?" Addressing reasoning and sense making does not need to be an extra burden for teachers struggling with students who are having a difficult time just learning the procedures. On the contrary, the structure that reasoning brings forms a vital support for understanding and continued learning. Currently, many students have difficulty because they find mathematics meaningless. Without the connections that reasoning and sense making provide, a seemingly endless cycle of reteaching may result. With purposeful attention and planning, teachers can hold all students in every high school mathematics classroom accountable for personally engaging in reasoning and sense making, and thus lead students to experience reasoning for themselves rather than merely observe it. Moreover, technology should be used strategically throughout the high school curriculum to help reach this goal; this point is addressed further in chapter 2.

What exactly do reasoning and sense making involve in the mathematics classroom? The following example shows how reasoning and sense making can be infused into teaching a formula that many students often regard as meaningless and hard to remember, the distance formula. The first scenario illustrates what frequently happens when students are asked to recall a procedure taught without understanding.

Teacher: Today's lesson requires that we calculate the distance between the center of a circle and a point on the circle in order to determine the circle's radius. Who remembers how to find the distance between two points?

Student 1: Isn't there a formula for that?

Student 2: I think it's x_1 plus x_2 squared, or something like that.

Student 1: Oh, yeah, I remember—there's a great big square root sign, but I don't remember what goes under it.

Student 3: I know! It's x_1 plus x_2 all over 2, isn't it?

Student 4: No, that's the midpoint formula.

(The discussion continues along these lines until the teacher reminds the class of the formula.)

The next year, this teacher decides to try a different approach that will engage the students in solving a problem. In the following scenario, we see students reasoning about mathematics, connecting what they are learning with their existing knowledge, and making sense of what the distance formula means.

Teacher: Let's take a look at a situation in which we need to find the distance between two locations on a map. Suppose this map shows your school; your house, which is located two blocks west and five blocks north of school; and your best friend's house, which is located eight blocks east and one block south of school. If the city had a system of evenly spaced perpendicular streets, how many blocks would we have to drive to get from your house to your friend's house?

Student 1: Well, we would have to drive ten blocks to the east and six blocks to the south, so I guess it would be sixteen blocks, right?

Teacher: Now, what if you could use a helicopter to fly straight to your friend's house? How could we find the distance "as the crow flies"? Work with your partners to establish a coordinate-axis system and show the path you'd have to drive to get to your friend's house. Next, work on calculating the direct distance between the houses if you could fly.

Student 1: What if we use the school as the origin? Then wouldn't my house be at $(-2, 5)$ and my friend's house, at $(8, -1)$?

Student 2:   Yeah, that sounds right. Here, let's draw the path on the streets connecting the two houses and then draw a line segment connecting the two houses.

Student 1:   Maybe we could measure the length of a block and find the distance with a ruler.

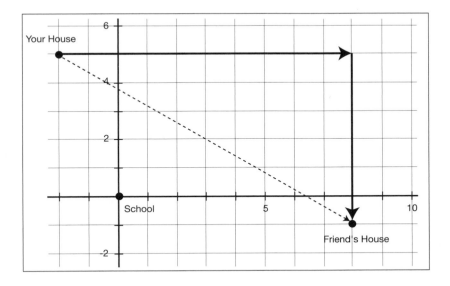

Student 3:   Wait a minute—you just drew a right triangle, because the streets are perpendicular.

Student 4:   So that means we could use the Pythagorean theorem: $10^2 + 6^2 = c^2$, so $c = \sqrt{136}$.

Student 2:   But how many blocks would that be?

Student 3:   Shouldn't the distance be between eleven and twelve blocks, since $121 < 136 < 144$? Actually, it's probably closer to twelve blocks, since 136 is much closer to 144.

(The teacher then extends the discussion to consider other examples and finally to develop a general formula.)

By having her students approach the distance formula from a reasoning-and-sense-making perspective the second year, the teacher increases their understanding of the formula and why it is true, increasing the likelihood that they will be able to retrieve, or quickly recreate, the formula at a later time.

Conclusion

Reasoning and sense making are the cornerstones of mathematics. Restructuring the high school mathematics program around them enhances students' development of both the content and process knowledge they need to be successful in their continuing study of mathematics and in their lives.

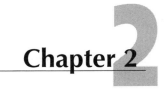

Chapter 2

Reasoning Habits

*Reasoning and sense making should be a part of
the mathematics classroom every day.*

A FOCUS on reasoning and sense making implies that "covering" mathematical topics is not enough. Students also need to experience and develop mathematical reasoning habits (cf. Cuoco, Goldenberg, and Mark [1996]; Driscoll [1999]; Pólya [1952, 1957]; Schoenfeld [1983]; Harel and Sowder [2005]). A *reasoning habit* is a productive way of thinking that becomes common in the processes of mathematical inquiry and sense making. The following list of reasoning habits illustrates the types of thinking that should become routine and fully expected in the classroom culture of all mathematics classes across all levels of high school.

Approaching the list as a new set of topics to be taught in an already crowded curriculum is not likely to have the desired effect. Instead, attention to reasoning habits needs to be integrated within the curriculum to ensure that students both understand and can use what they are taught.

- *Analyzing a problem,* for example,
    - *identifying relevant* mathematical *concepts, procedures, or representations* that reveal important information about the problem and contribute to its solution (for example, choosing a model for simulating a random experiment);
    - *defining relevant variables and conditions* carefully, including units if appropriate;
    - *seeking patterns and relationships* (for example, systematically examining cases or creating displays for data);
    - *looking for hidden structure* (for example, drawing auxiliary lines in geometric figures or finding equivalent forms of expressions that reveal different aspects of a problem);
    - *considering special cases or simpler analogs;*
    - *applying previously learned concepts* to new problem situations, adapting and extending as necessary;
    - *making preliminary deductions and conjectures,* including predicting what a solution to a problem might involve or putting constraints on solutions; and
    - *deciding whether a statistical approach is appropriate.*

- *Implementing a strategy,* for example,
  - — *making purposeful use of procedures;*
  - — *organizing the solution,* including calculations, algebraic manipulations, and data displays;
  - — *making logical deductions* based on current progress, verifying conjectures, and extending initial findings; and
  - — *monitoring progress toward a solution,* including reviewing a chosen strategy and other possible strategies generated by oneself or others.

- *Seeking and using connections* across different mathematical domains, different contexts, and different representations.

- *Reflecting on a solution* to a problem, for example,
  - — *interpreting a solution* and how it answers the problem, including making decisions under uncertain conditions;
  - — *considering the reasonableness of a solution*, including whether any numbers are reported at an unreasonable level of accuracy;
  - — *revisiting initial assumptions* about the nature of the solution, including being mindful of special cases and extraneous solutions;
  - — *justifying or validating a solution*, including through proof or inferential reasoning;
  - — *recognizing the scope of inference* for a statistical solution;
  - — *reconciling different approaches* to solving the problem, including those proposed by others;
  - — *refining arguments* so that they can be effectively communicated; and
  - — *generalizing a solution* to a broader class of problems and looking for connections with other problems.

Many of these reasoning habits could be construed to fit in more than one category, and students are expected to move naturally among various reasoning habits as they are needed. Section 2 of this publication offers examples of how reasoning habits can be promoted in the high school classroom, with specific references to the reasoning habits listed above.

Progression of Reasoning

When reasoning is interwoven with sense making, and when teachers provide the necessary support and formative feedback, students can be expected to demonstrate growing levels of formality in their reasoning in the classroom, in their oral and written work, and in assessments throughout the high school years. Reasoning and sense making in the high school mathematics classroom require increasing levels of understanding, as outlined in the following:

empirical— the role of empirical evidence that supports, but does not justify, a conjecture— "it works in a number of cases";

preformal— the role of intuitive explanations and partial arguments that lend insight into what is happening; and *formal—* the role of formal argumentation (based on logic) in determining mathematical certainty (proof) or in making statistical inferences.

Thus, these levels show progress from less formal reasoning to more formal reasoning. However, each level has value. Students may continually shift among these levels, even within the same mathematical context. This shifting among levels is not only expected but desirable as students make sense of the context and reason their way to a conclusion. However, teachers play an essential role in encouraging students to explore more sophisticated levels of reasoning and sense making.

Formal argumentation includes both the ability of students to create meaningful chains of logical reasoning based on certain assumptions, definitions, and prior results, as well as the ability to read and evaluate reasoning given by others. The ability to determine the validity of an argument is important, as is an understanding of what the argument says about the ideas under consideration.

Developing Reasoning Habits in the Classroom

Teachers can help students progress to higher levels of reasoning through judicious selection of tasks and the use of probing questions. Students can then learn to analyze their approach to solving problems, recognize the strengths and shortcomings of their current approach, and use the power of more formal reasoning to better formulate and justify mathematical conclusions. The continuing development of mathematical reasoning habits should be a priority in the high school classroom. The following is a preliminary list of tips for developing these habits.

- Provide tasks that require students to figure things out for themselves.
- Ask students to restate the problem in their own words, including any assumptions they have made.
- Give students time to analyze a problem intuitively, explore the problem further by using models, and then proceed to a more formal approach.
- Resist the urge to tell students how to solve a problem when they become frustrated; find other ways to support students as they think and work.
- Ask students questions that will prompt their thinking—for example, "Why does this work?" or "How do you know?"
- Provide adequate wait time after a question for students to formulate their own reasoning.
- Encourage students to ask probing questions of themselves and one another.
- Expect students to communicate their reasoning to their classmates and the teacher, orally and in writing, through using proper mathematical vocabulary.
- Highlight exemplary explanations, and have students reflect on what makes them effective.
- Establish a classroom climate in which students feel comfortable sharing their mathematical arguments and critiquing the arguments of others in a productive manner.

Teachers should refer to other resources for specific tasks, suggestions for questioning techniques, and so forth. NCTM and other professional organizations offer a number of valuable resources, both in print and online. Additional teaching ideas related to reasoning and sense making are also presented in more detail in the topic books that support this publication.

Reasoning as the Foundation of Mathematical Competence

Reasoning and sense making are inherent in developing mathematical competence, as discussed in *Adding It Up* (Kilpatrick, Swafford, and Findell 2001); see figure 2.1. Sense making and conceptual understanding are closely interrelated. Procedural fluency includes learning with understanding and knowing which procedure to choose, when to choose it, and for what purpose. In the absence of reasoning, students may carry out procedures correctly but may also capriciously invoke incorrect or baseless rules, such as "the square root of a sum is the sum of the square roots." They come to view procedures as steps they are told to do rather than a series of steps chosen for a specific purpose and based on mathematical principles. Without developing an understanding of procedures rooted in reasoning and sense making, students may be able to correctly perform those procedures but may think of them only as a list of "tricks." As a result, they may have difficulty selecting an appropriate procedure to use in a given problem, or their seeming competence with simple tasks may evaporate in more complicated situations. Genuine procedural fluency requires both mastering technical skills and developing the understanding needed for using them appropriately. Strategic competence and adaptive reasoning are both directly addressed in the reasoning habits.

Conceptual understanding —	comprehension of mathematical concepts, operations, and relations
Procedural fluency —	skill in carrying out procedures flexibly, accurately, efficiently, and appropriately.
Strategic competence —	ability to formulate, represent, and solve mathematical problems
Adaptive reasoning —	capacity for logical thought, reflection, explanation, and justification
Productive disposition —	habitual inclination to see mathematics as sensible, useful, and worthwhile, coupled with a belief in diligence and one's own efficacy

Fig. 2.1. The strands of mathematical proficiency from *Adding It Up*
(Kilpatrick, Swafford, and Findell 2001)

The development of a "productive disposition" (Kilpatrick, Swafford, and Findell 2001) is a high priority of all school mathematics programs. When students achieve this goal, they view mathematics as a reasoning and sense-making enterprise. This goal can be achieved only if students personally engage in mathematical reasoning and sense making as they learn mathematics content.

Statistical Reasoning

Statistical reasoning involves making interpretations based on, and inferences from, data. Statistics furnishes tools for investigating questions by providing strategies for collecting useful data, methods for analyzing the data, and unique perspectives for interpreting the meaning of the data within the context of the problem. The need for statistics arises from "the omnipresence of variability" in data (Cobb and Moore 1997, p. 801), and statistical reasoning uses a combination of ideas from both data and chance in seeking to understand that variability. Such notions as distribution, center, spread, association, uncertainty, randomness, sampling, and statistical experiments are foundational concepts underlying the development of statistical reasoning.

Statistics is increasingly recognized as essential for students' success in dealing with the requirements of citizenship, employment, and continuing education (Franklin et al. 2007; College Board 2006, 2007; American Diploma Project 2004). Consequently, the development of statistical reasoning must be a high priority for school mathematics. Garfield (2002) describes a developmental model portraying five stages of statistical reasoning for students, from its lowest level of *idiosyncratic reasoning* (use of some statistical terms without full understanding) to its highest level of *integrated process reasoning* (complete understanding of a statistical process). Preparing high school graduates with the ability to make sense of data, and with the capacity to reason with statistics at the integrated process level, requires that students be engaged with meaningful activities involving data and chance throughout prekindergarten through grade 12.

Mathematical Modeling

The tools and reasoning processes of mathematics help us understand and operate in the physical and social worlds. Mathematical modeling involves a process of connecting mathematics with a real-world situation; figure 2.2 outlines a cycle often used to organize reasoning in mathematical modeling. A mathematical model is essentially an axiomatization of some sliver of the real world to be able to deal with it mathematically. The connections between mathematics and real-world problems developed in mathematical modeling add value to, and provide incentive and context for, studying mathematical topics.

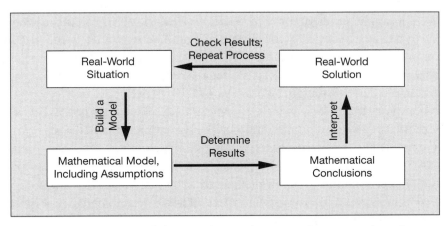

Fig. 2.2. Four-step modeling cycle used to organize reasoning about mathematical modeling

Several additional benefits can be realized from modeling, as can be seen in several examples in section 2. First, mathematical modeling also offers opportunities to make reasoned connections among different mathematical arenas, because in many situations, real-world problems require a combination of mathematical tools. Example 17, "Clearing the Bridge," is a vivid example of how mathematical modeling can cross several mathematical strands. Second, modeling gives students an opportunity to combine mathematical ideas in novel ways. Not only is this ability a life skill, but the ability to use knowledge effectively in new situations has been highlighted in several reports on the workforce and innovation (Partnership for 21st Century Skills 2007; Secretary's Commission on Achieving Necessary Skills 1991; Association for Operations Management [APICS] 2001). Third, working to establish a mathematical model can allow students to become engrossed in the mathematics in ways that promote mathematical reasoning. Fourth, modeling can provide a contextual need to *develop* mathematical ideas as well as apply them. For example, creating an animation by modeling the movement of images in a plane can serve as motivation to introduce and study matrix theory. Fifth, modeling situations can provide points of access for learners with various backgrounds and skills. Many modeling examples can be continued to very advanced levels. For instance, example 17, "Clearing the Bridge," can be extended into the calculus classroom. Finally, as exemplified by example 14, "Picture This," some modeling contexts can serve as the bases of several lessons—reflecting the genuine fact that persistent, extended efforts are sometimes needed to solve mathematics problems.

Technology to Support Reasoning and Sense Making

Technology is an integral part of society, the workplace, and even many areas of modern mathematical research itself (Bailey and Borwein 2005); the mathematics classroom needs to reflect that reality. Technology can be used to advance the goals of reasoning and sense making in the high school mathematics classroom. Technological tools can be particularly useful in looking for patterns and relationships and in forming conjectures—see examples 9, "More Than Meets the Eye"; 14, "Picture This"; and 17, "Clearing the Bridge." Technology can relieve students of burdensome computations, giving them the freedom, and the need, to think strategically, as in example 9, "More Than Meets the Eye." Using technology to display multiple representations of the same problem can aid in making connections, as in example 11, "Take As Directed." When technology allows multiple representations to be linked dynamically, it can provide new opportunities for students to take mathematically meaningful actions and immediately see mathematically meaningful consequences—fertile ground for sense-making and reasoning activities. This dynamic linking is evident in example 13, "Tidal Waves." Technology can also be useful in generalizing a solution, as in example 22, "Meaningful Words, Part B."

The incorporation of technology in the classroom should not overshadow the development of the procedural proficiency needed by students to support continued mathematical growth. It should be used as a tool that leads to a deeper understanding of mathematical concepts. Students can be challenged to take responsibility for deciding which tool might be useful in a given situation when they are allowed to choose from a menu of mathematical tools that includes technology. Students who have regular opportunities to discuss and reflect on how a technological tool is used effectively will be less apt to use technology as a crutch.

Conclusion

Reasoning and sense making must become a part of the fabric of the high school mathematics classroom. Not only are they important goals themselves, but they are the foundation for true mathematical competence. Incorporating isolated experiences with reasoning and sense making will not suffice. Teachers must consistently support and encourage students' progress toward more sophisticated levels of reasoning.

Reasoning and Sense Making in the Curriculum

Chapter 3

Reasoning and Sense Making across the Curriculum

*Reasoning and sense making are integral to the
experiences of all students across all areas of the
high school mathematics curriculum.*

REASONING and sense making should be pervasive across all areas of the high school
mathematics curriculum. Although aspects of formal reasoning are frequently emphasized
in geometry, students are less likely to encounter reasoning in other areas of the curriculum, such
as algebra. When reasoning and sense making are infused throughout the curriculum, they lend coherence across the domains of mathematics—number, algebra, geometry, and statistics—whether
the curriculum is arranged in the customary U.S. course-based sequence (first-year algebra, geometry, second-year algebra) or in an integrated manner. A focus on reasoning also helps students see
how new concepts connect with existing knowledge.

We emphasize that we do not propose introducing "reasoning" as a set of topics to be added to
a crowded curriculum, but as a stance toward learning mathematics. Developing strong reasoning
habits will of course take instructional time. However, it also promises compensating efficiencies.
First, the initial part of each course that is frequently spent reteaching content from previous courses may be reduced if those courses emphasize reasoned connections with existing knowledge, so
that students are better able to retain what they have learned. Second, emphasizing the underlying
connections that promote reasoning and sense making introduces coherence that allows stream-
lining of the curriculum. As attention turns to how those underlying connections build across the
high school years, less time needs to be spent addressing lists of particular skills that need to be
mastered.

For example, teaching students to factor polynomials often consumes considerable time, as
students are taught methods for factoring (1) common monomial terms from a polynomial, (2)
trinomials with leading coefficient of 1 (with or without negative coefficients), (3) trinomials with
a leading coefficient other than 1 (which may eventually be a noninteger), (4) special cases, such
as perfect squares and the difference of squares (or cubes), and (5) more-complex trinomials in
which the exponent of the variable in one term is double that in another. Nonetheless, students who

are given experiences that help them see all these different forms as results of using the distributive law may be more likely to understand the common structure behind the different factoring methods, and thus develop fluency with them. The area model is particularly useful in visualizing the distributive law; see examples 4 and 8 for a discussion of area models. This approach may also facilitate long-term retention more effectively than teaching particular procedures for factoring in isolation.

The following chapters in this section illustrate how the high school mathematics curriculum can be focused on broad themes that promote reasoning and sense making within five specific content areas of the high school curriculum:

- Reasoning with Number and Measurement
- Reasoning with Algebraic Symbols
- Reasoning with Functions
- Reasoning with Geometry
- Reasoning with Statistics and Probability

Within each content area, a number of key elements provide a broad structure for thinking about how the content area can be focused on reasoning and sense making. These key elements are not intended to be an exhaustive list of specific topics to be addressed. Instead, they provide a lens through which to view the potential of high school programs for promoting and developing mathematical reasoning and sense making. The task of creating a curriculum that fully achieves the goals of this publication will be challenging. Although important content must be addressed, this task requires much more than developing lists of topics to be taught in a particular course.

Furthermore, those responsible for making decisions about the curriculum must be aware of the need to offer experiences with reasoning and sense making within a broad curriculum that meets the needs of a wide range of students, preparing them for future success as citizens and in the workplace, as well as for careers in mathematics and science. Hard choices will be need to made about the topics traditionally included in the curriculum to make room for areas that have often been underemphasized, such as statistics. Many examples exist of schools and teachers who have already begun to reexamine their curricular priorities and instructional emphases to maximize focus on reasoning and sense making for all students across the years of high school mathematics. All schools and teachers must begin, or continue, this journey.

Discrete mathematics, an active branch of contemporary mathematics that is widely used in business and industry, is an additional area of mathematics that is addressed in this publication. We argue that discrete mathematics should be an integral part of the school mathematics curriculum (NCTM 2000a). As in *Principles and Standards*, the main topics of discrete mathematics are distributed throughout the strands rather than receive separate treatment, as shown in figure 3.1.

Attention to discrete mathematics is embedded in the following strands of *Focus in High School Mathematics:*

- Counting is incorporated as a key element within Reasoning with Number and Measurement and is addressed in example 20, "What Are the Chances? Part A."
- Recursion is included in the "Multiple representations of functions" key element of Reasoning with Functions; see example 11, "Take As Directed."
- Vertex-edge graphs are addressed in the last key element of Reasoning with Geometry; see example 18, "Assigning Frequencies."

Fig. 3.1. Discrete mathematics in *Focus in High School Mathematics*

The following chapters describe how reasoning and sense making can be promoted within the five content areas outlined above and characterize the key elements in each content area. These chapters include a series of examples in a variety of formats—including classroom vignettes and assessment items, as well as mathematical exposition. The examples are intended to provide an idealized illustration of how reasoning and sense making might unfold in high school mathematics.

Chapter 4

Reasoning with Number and Measurement

MUCH of mathematics, particularly the domains of number and measurement, originated in efforts to quantify the world. Number and measurement, which receive substantial attention in kindergarten through grade 8, are foundational for high school mathematics; without reasoning skills in these areas, students will be limited in their reasoning in other areas of mathematics.

Key elements of reasoning and sense making with number and measurement include the following:

- *Reasonableness of answers and measurements.* Judging whether a given answer or measurement has an appropriate order of magnitude, and whether it is expressed in appropriate units.

- *Approximations and error.* Realizing that all real-world measurements are approximations and that unsuitably accurate values should not be used for real-world quantities; recognizing the role of error in subsequent computations with measurements.

- *Number systems.* Understanding number-system properties deeply; extending number-system properties to algebraic situations.

- *Counting.* Recognizing when enumeration would be a productive approach to solving a problem, and then using principles and techniques of counting to find a solution.

We address these key elements in more detail in the following sections.

Reasonableness of Answers and Measurements

Students should possess "number sense" related to the base-ten numeration system. They should know that the leading, or leftmost, digit of a number accounts for most of the number, and that the digits to the right of the leading two or three digits of a measurement are "loose change" and are often insignificant. For example, although the U.S. Census Bureau Web site reports that the world population was 6,752,904,311 as of 9:48 a.m. on January 10, 2009, this number is only a rough estimate based on data provided from nations around the world. Indeed, one can often use round numbers to do approximate calculations that will yield simple but fairly accurate approximations of quantities of interest. See, for example, the comments of student 3 in example 1. This example also shows the importance of justifying one's answer and considering whether a solution makes sense and answers the question.

Example 1: Around the World

Task

Estimate the total surface area of the earth.

In the Classroom (Geometry Class)

Teacher: What would you predict the total surface area of the earth is?

Student 1: Wow, I would have no idea. I'd guess either a million or maybe a billion square miles.

Student 2: Well, it is a ball, which is basically a sphere. So if we knew the radius, I guess we could figure that out.

Teacher: OK, to help you out, I'll tell you that its radius is about 4,000 miles.

Student 2: So then $A = 4\pi r^2$, and we just need to plug the radius in.

Student 3: If the radius is about 4 thousand, then squaring will take us to about 16 million. And 4π is a little more than 12, and $12 \times 16 = 192$, so I'll guess maybe 200 million square miles.

Student 4: Yeah, that's decent, but why not just use the π-button on your calculator? That's what I did, and I got 201,061,930.

Teacher: So which do you think is the best estimate?

Student 4: Mine, because it's most accurate.

Student 3: But we don't know exactly what the radius of the earth is. Besides, the earth may not be exactly spherical. Your number is within 1 percent of 200,000,000, so I think 200,000,000 is good enough.

Key Elements of Mathematics

Reasoning with Number and Measurement—Reasonableness of answers and measurements; Approximations and error

Reasoning Habits

Analyzing a problem—making preliminary deductions and conjectures

Reflecting on a solution—considering the reasonableness of a solution; justifying or validating a solution

Number sense lays an important foundation for learning high school mathematics. The National Mathematics Advisory Panel (2008) noted that "poor number sense interferes with learning algorithms and number facts and prevents the use of strategies to verify if solutions to problems are reasonable" (p. 27). The report goes on to identify the importance of developing both conceptual and procedural knowledge of fractions for progress in mathematics and the "pervasive difficulties" (p. 28) that students have. Although instructional time precludes reteaching the number concepts and operations that students should already have learned as they enter high school, attention to number sense can profitably be integrated into instructional objectives at the high school level. For example, teachers might routinely ask students to decide whether an answer to a given computation has the right order of magnitude, or what degree of accuracy would be appropriate in an answer, and to then state the reasoning for their judgment.

In this publication, we call for the extension of "number sense" at the high school level to new sets of numbers and situations. Students should develop intuitions about situations involving radicals and negative and fractional exponents. For example, when calculating $12^{\frac{3}{2}}$, a student might reason that because 12 is between 9 and 16, $12^{\frac{1}{2}}$ must be between 3 and 4. Because $12^{\frac{3}{2}} = 12^1 \cdot 12^{\frac{1}{2}}$, the answer should be between 36 and 48. Thus, if a student enters "12^3/2" into his or her calculator to compute $12^{\frac{3}{2}}$ and gets an answer of 864, he or she should immediately realize that a mistake has been made.

When working with measurements, students should have a sense of what units are appropriate for the solution to a problem. Example 2 presents a class discussion in which the teacher facilitates a comparison of different solutions to a problem. To help students interpret how their solutions might answer the problem, the teacher asks them to write out a formal response to the problem.

Example 2: Fuel for Thought

Task

A teacher gives her students the following quiz taken from an article in the *New York Times* (Chang 2008) and asks them to explain their reasoning:

Quiz time: Which of the following would save more fuel?
a) Replacing a compact car that gets 34 miles per gallon (MPG) with a hybrid that gets 54 MPG.
b) Replacing a sport utility vehicle (SUV) that gets 18 MPG with a sedan that gets 28 MPG.
c) Both changes save the same amount of fuel.

In the Classroom (First-Year Algebra)

The teacher collects the quizzes and asks two of her students to share their answers with the class. The first student responds:

> I would say the correct answer is (a). My reasoning is that the change from 34 MPG to 54 is an increase of about 59 percent, but the 18 to 28 MPG change is an increase of only about 56 percent.

The second student responds:

> I thought about how much gas it would take to make a 100-mile trip.
>
> *Considering the compact car:*
>
> 100 miles/54 MPG = 1.85 gallons used.
>
> 100 miles/34 MPG = 2.94 gallons used.

Example 2: Fuel for Thought—*Continued*

So switching from a 34 MPG to a 54 MPG car would save 1.09 gallons of gas.

Looking at the SUV:

100 miles/28 MPG = 3.57 gallons used.

100 miles/18 MPG = 5.56 gallons used.

So switching from an 18 MPG car to a 28 MPG car saves 1.99 gallons of gas every 100 miles. That means you are actually saving more gas by replacing the SUV.

The teacher then asks the class to compare these two responses. After a spirited debate among students who had chosen each of the answers, the class reaches a consensus that both responses had merit, depending on how the problem is interpreted. Although the fuel efficiency increased slightly more for the compact car, the owner would actually save more gallons of gasoline by replacing the SUV if both cars were driven the same number of miles.

The teacher asks the class to explore the relationship of MPG with actual gasoline consumption. After the students work in small groups for a few minutes, the teacher asks one group to show the table of values and graph it has made, as shown below. They explain, "You save less fuel as you go up another 5 MPG over and over. So as we saw in the quiz, MPG can be a little confusing."

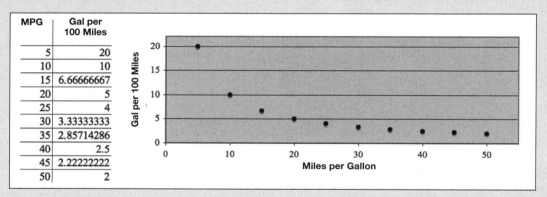

MPG	Gal per 100 Miles
5	20
10	10
15	6.66666667
20	5
25	4
30	3.33333333
35	2.85714286
40	2.5
45	2.22222222
50	2

The teacher then gives the class the article from the *New York Times* from which the quiz was taken to read for homework, along with some online comments from readers. She asks the students to analyze the arguments from the article in a brief essay and to propose what unit of measure they think will be useful for comparing the fuel consumption of cars.

One group made this report: "The low mileage cars offer more opportunities for savings because they are using so much gas. If you go from 10 MPG to 20 MPG, you go from using 10 gallons for 100 miles to 5 gallons. You have saved 5 gallons per hundred miles, and that is as much as you are using after the improvement. If you double the rate again to 40 MPG, you will still use 2½ gallons in 100 miles, so you have only saved 2½ gallons from the 20 MPG amount or 7½ gallons from the 10 MPG amount. Even if you double again, to 80 MPG, you

---

Example 2: Fuel for Thought—*Continued*

will still use 1.25 gallons, so you have only saved an additional 1.25 gallons from the 40 MPG amount. The point seems to be, the less you use, the less savings you have available. You can't save more than you use."

Key Elements of Mathematics

Reasoning with Number and Measurement—Reasonableness of answers and measurements

Reasoning with Functions—Multiple representations of functions

Reasoning Habits

Analyzing a problem—seeking patterns and relationships

Reflecting on a solution—interpreting a solution; reconciling different approaches; refining arguments

---

Approximations and Error

Pure mathematics is exact, but when we want to apply it to the world, we must learn to cope with approximation. Numbers obtained through measurement rather than counting are subject to error, an important concept with which students need to struggle (Lehrer 2003). "Error" does not mean "mistake"; it is the unavoidable inexactness that is inherent in all real-world situations. Many high school students have not grasped the significance of reporting their measure to the nearest unit or subunit of measurement, depending on the measuring device. Moreover, the accuracy of the measurement affects any results that are subsequently reported. When scientists give results based on measurements—often a mixture of direct and computed measures—they are careful to report the method(s) used to obtain them. Students should realize that in a measurement, the digits beyond the first few are likely not relevant and that they should be suspicious when they see measurements with many decimal places in news reports. Students should learn that the accuracy of a result can be more effectively specified using the idea of *relative error*. Relative error is illustrated in example 3, as is the need for students to monitor their progress and adjust their strategies accordingly.

Example 3: Around Pi

Task

Although we know that π is an irrational number, we often use such approximations as 3.14 or 22/7. How much error are we introducing by using such an approximation? Find an upper bound for the relative error, and illustrate with a specific example.

Example 3: Around Pi—*Continued*

In the Classroom (Second-Year Algebra)

Helping students move beyond the notion of error as a mistake is an important part of the sense-making process for a productive discussion of error. Students may view error as *how far they are from a correct answer.* The teacher can build on this view to discus *error* as the difference between an approximation (v) and the "real" value (V), and *absolute error* as the absolute value or magnitude of the error, $|V - v|$. Developing an understanding of *relative error* as a percent of the "real" value can help students make sense of the formula for relative error, $\dfrac{|V-v|}{V}$. To better understand his students' progress in understanding relative error, a teacher assigns the "Around Pi" task as an in-class assessment to be completed individually. One student's response follows, with the teacher's comments in the margin:

> I usually use 3.14, so I decided to try that in the formula. But when I tried to figure out $|V-v|$, I got confused since we don't have an actual value for V. But then I got this idea that I can be sure it is less than .0016, since π < 3.14159.... So then I thought about $\dfrac{|V-v|}{V \leftarrow (big\ V)}$. We still don't know what π is, but since V is in the denominator, I'll pick something ~~bigger~~ *less* than V, which would be 3.141₆. So $\dfrac{.0016}{3.141₅} = 5.0929 × 10^{-4}$. That's really small! Then I tried this with the area of a circle, with radius 5, using 3.14 and the π button on my calculator, and it was only off by about .0399, so I guess that's pretty good!

Great idea! But you could explain this a little more fully

Why did you change to less? Why was that important?

Is this the exact value? Continue your argument using bounds.

Is this relative error? Have you really made your point with this example?

How does using the π button relate to the value of V?

Key Elements of Mathematics

Reasoning with Number and Measurement—Approximations and error

Reasoning Habits

Analyzing a problem—defining relevant variables and conditions
Implementing a strategy—monitoring progress toward a solution
Reflecting on a solution—justifying or validating a solution; refining arguments

Number Systems

A solid understanding of number systems and their properties sets a foundation for meaningful development of algebra (Carraher and Schliemann 2007). Example 4 illustrates how an understanding of the distributive property with multidigit multiplication forms the basis for multiplication of polynomials; this point is further elaborated in example 6, "Distribute Thoroughly."

Example 4: A Model Idea

Background

The distributive property can be illustrated with an *area model*. Take, for example, the product of 62 and 43. If each factor is written in expanded form, we have

$$(62)(43) = (60 + 2)(40 + 3) = 24(100) + 18(10) + 8(10) + 6.$$

The figure below shows groups of 100, 10, and 1 represented geometrically, helping students make sense not only of the distributive property but also of perfect squares and orders of magnitude.

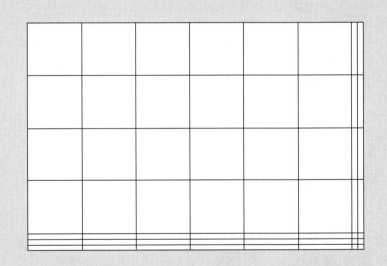

Once the concept of using area to model multiplication of integers has been established, ideally in kindergarten–grade 8, area models can help students make sense of many processes, such as multiplication of fractions and polynomials.

Task

The distributive property for multiplication of variables can be modeled for such expressions as $A(B + C)$. As shown in the figure that follows, $AB + AC = A(B + C)$.

Example 4: A Model Idea—Continued

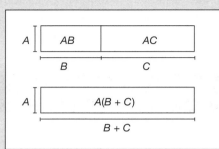

Create an area model for the product $(x + 3)(x + y + 5)$.

In the Classroom (First-Year Algebra)

Students could create area models by drawing on graph paper or using algebra tiles. Two possible area models are shown below. The first shows regions of area x^2, xy, x, y, and 1. By counting the number of each type of region present (i.e., one group of x^2, three groups of y, and so forth), students can make sense of what each term in the expansion of the product represents. The second model shows the area of each smaller rectangular region as the product of its dimensions. This type of area model illustrates that the sum of the smaller areas (products of terms) is equal to the area of the original factors, thus forming a connection with the area addition postulate.

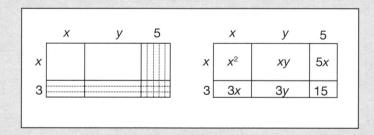

Key Elements of Mathematics

Reasoning with Number and Measurement—Number systems

Reasoning Habits

Analyzing a problem—identifying relevant concepts, procedures, or representations; applying previously learned concepts

Seeking and using connections

Counting

Counting principles and techniques, an important topic from discrete mathematics, have applications both within and outside mathematics. See example 20, "What Are the Chances? Part A" for an application of counting principles to probability models. Students need to understand the difference between counting the number of possible outcomes and enumerating all possible cases. For example, when rolling a pair of dice and summing the numbers of the topmost faces, eleven sums from 2 to 12 are possible. Yet not all sums are equally likely, because five ways exist to get 6 (1 + 5, 2 + 4, 3 + 3, 4 + 2, and 5 + 1) but only one way to get 2 (1 + 1). Another important counting skill is understanding the difference between situations in which the order of events matters (e.g., the digits in a number) and situations in which order is irrelevant (e.g., membership on a committee, as in example 20, "What Are the Chances? Part A").

A solid understanding of number and measurement continues to be important at the high school level because it provides the foundation for reasoning about other mathematical concepts. Helping students make sense of these essential ideas will ease their transition to more abstract topics.

Chapter 5

Reasoning with Algebraic Symbols

THE algebraic notation we use today is a major accomplishment of humankind, allowing for the compact representation of complex calculations and problems (Fey 1984; Radford and Puig 2007). However, that very compactness can be a barrier to sense making (Radford and Puig 2007; Saul 2001). A basic task for teachers of algebra is to help students reason their way through that barrier.

Key elements of reasoning and sense making with algebraic symbols include the following:

- *Meaningful use of symbols.* Choosing variables and constructing expressions and equations in context; interpreting the form of expressions and equations; manipulating expressions so that interesting interpretations can be made.

- *Mindful manipulation.* Connecting manipulation with the laws of arithmetic; anticipating the results of manipulations; choosing procedures purposefully in context; picturing calculations mentally.

- *Reasoned solving.* Seeing solution steps as logical deductions about equality; interpreting solutions in context.

- *Connecting algebra with geometry.* Representing geometric situations algebraically and algebraic situations geometrically; using connections in solving problems.

- *Linking expressions and functions.* Using multiple algebraic representations to understand functions; working with function notation.

We address these key elements in more detail in the following sections.

Meaningful Use of Symbols

Meaningful use of symbols includes carefully defining the meaning of symbols introduced to solve problems, including specifying units and distinguishing among the three main uses of variables—(1) as unknowns (e.g., find the value of Q such that $3Q - 4 = 11$), (2) as placeholders that can take on a range of values (e.g., $a + c = c + a$ for all a and c), and (3) as parameters of a function (e.g., What is the effect of increasing m on the graph of $y = mx + b$?) (Usiskin 1988).

Although a long-term goal of algebraic learning is a fluid, nearly automatic facility with manipulating algebraic expressions that might seem to resemble what is often called "mindless manipulation," this ease can best be achieved by first learning to pay close attention to interpreting expressions, both at a formal level and as statements about real-world situations. At the outset, the reasons and justifications for forming and manipulating expressions should be major emphases of instruction (Kaput, Blanton, and Moreno 2008). As comfort with expressions grows, constructing and interpreting them require less and less effort and gradually become almost subconscious. The true foundation for algebraic manipulation is close attention to meaning and structure.

Reasoning with algebraic expressions depends on being able to read them in different ways, for example, seeing $3 - (4 - x)^2$ as 3 minus a quantity squared and thus as a value less than or equal to 3, as a function of $4 - x$, and as a function of x. In example 5 students are asked to interpret the purposes of different forms of the same expression.

Example 5: Horseshoes in Flight

Task

The height of a thrown horseshoe depends on the time that has elapsed since its release, as shown in the graph. Note that this graph is parabolic, but it may not be the same as the graph of the horseshoe's path. Its height (measured in feet) as a function of time (measured in seconds) from the instant of release is

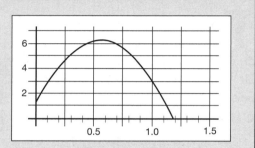

$$1\frac{3}{16} + 18t - 16t^2.$$

The expressions (a)–(d) below are equivalent. Which is most useful for finding the maximum height of the horseshoe, and why is it the most useful expression?

(a) $1\frac{3}{16} + 18t - 16t^2$ (b) $-16(t - \frac{19}{16})(t + \frac{1}{16})$

(c) $\frac{1}{16}(19 - 16t)(16t + 1)$ (d) $-16(t - \frac{9}{16})^2 + \frac{100}{16}$

In the Classroom (Second-Year Algebra)

Group report: We eliminated expression (a). It tells us the starting height and starting upward speed, but the question is not about either of those. Expressions (b) and (c) are pretty much the same, except that the denominators in the factors have been pulled out in front in (c). One of us used (b) to find the zeros ($\frac{19}{16}$ and $-\frac{1}{16}$), and then found the midpoint ($\frac{9}{16}$), which should be the time at which the maximum height is achieved. But we finally decided on (d) because the term

$$-16(t - \frac{9}{16})^2$$

is always negative or zero, so we could see that the height never goes above $\frac{100}{16}$ feet, or $6\frac{1}{4}$ feet, and that it reaches this height at $t = \frac{9}{16}$ seconds, which is the same as the midpoint found by using (b).

Example 5: Horseshoes in Flight—*Continued*

Key Elements of Mathematics

Reasoning with Algebraic Symbols—Meaningful use of symbols; Linking expressions and functions

Reasoning Habits

Analyzing a problem—looking for hidden structure
Reflecting on a solution—interpreting a solution; justifying or validating a solution

---

Example 5 also raises a common difficulty to which teachers may need to be sensitive—confusion between a representation of the actual flight of an object (in this instance a horseshoe) and the time-versus-height graph. To help clarify this issue, teachers might ask such questions as "How far do you think the horseshoe would travel?" (certainly more than 1.2 feet) or "How do the scales of the two axes compare?"

Mindful Manipulation

Mindful manipulation includes learning algebraic manipulation as a process guided by understanding and goals (how do I want to use this expression, and what will make it most useful for this purpose?) and seeing that the basic rules of arithmetic provide a rationale for all legitimate manipulations of polynomial expressions. Of these, the distributive property, which is the only rule connecting the operations of addition and multiplication, is the one to which we must constantly appeal when doing anything that involves both operations at once, including a wide range of manipulations: expanding, factoring, collecting like terms, and putting fractions over a common denominator. Example 6 illustrates the difference between mindless and mindful manipulation when multiplying polynomials. It also illustrates the importance of organizing one's solution.

Example 6: Distribute Thoroughly

Task

Expand:

(a) $(1 + x^3)(1 + x + x^2)$

(b) $(1 + x)(1 + x + x^2)$

In the Classroom (First-Year Algebra)

Student 1 is accustomed to using the mnemonic FOIL (First, Outer, Inner, Last) to expand products of two binomials, such as $(1 + x)(1 + x^2)$, and applies it to the problem

Example 6: Distribute Thoroughly—*Continued*

$(1 + x^3)(1 + x + x^2)$, getting $1 + x^2 + x^3 + x^5$.

Student 2 says, "You missed the products of the middle term, x, in the second factor. The distributive property means we have to multiply each term of one factor with each term of the other, and then add all the products.

"So I get

$$(1 + x^3)(1 + x + x^2) = 1 \cdot 1 + 1 \cdot x + 1 \cdot x^2 + x^3 \cdot 1 + x^3 \cdot x + x^3 \cdot x^2$$
$$= 1 + x + x^2 + x^3 + x^4 + x^5.$$

"I sometimes remember this as 'each with each.' Sometimes you can just multiply the terms mentally. I like to visualize the steps and write as little as possible. For example, when I apply 'each with each' to

$$(1 - x)(1 + x + x^2) = 1 + x + x^2 - x - x^2 - x^3 = 1 - x^3,$$

I can see that the second and third terms from the multiplication by 1 are opposites of the first and second terms from multiplication by $-x$, so I can just write down the remaining terms."

Key Elements of Mathematics

Reasoning with Algebraic Symbols—Meaningful use of symbols; Mindful manipulation
Reasoning with Numbers and Measurements—Number systems

Reasoning Habits

Analyzing a problem—applying previously learned concepts
Implementing a strategy—making purposeful use of procedures; organizing the solution
Seeking and using connections

Reasoned Solving

Equation solving is a goal-oriented process of logical argument; it is based on general principles of equality and procedures of algebraic manipulation consistent with the rules of arithmetic. Problem solving with equations should include careful attention to increasingly difficult problems that span the border between arithmetic and algebra. Such problems can help students view algebra as a sense-making activity that extends one's problem-solving skills into domains in which reasoning as done in arithmetic becomes too complicated or cumbersome to carry out. Seeing the essential parallels between algebraic and arithmetic solution methods can help students realize that algebra is not something totally new but simply a more powerful tool for dealing with problems that are hard to approach with arithmetic by itself (Saul 2001). In example 7 we illustrate reasoned solving of equations. Worth noting is the fact that although one student used a standard algebraic approach and the other used reasoning based on the concrete context, the steps in their solutions are essentially the same. Examples of this sort can help students see algebra as an extension of concrete arithmetic reasoning.

Example 7: Finding Balance

Task

A slab of soap on one pan of a scale balances $\frac{3}{4}$ of a slab of soap of equal weight and a $\frac{3}{4}$-pound weight on the other pan. How much does the slab of soap weigh? Solve the problem both with an algebraic equation and by direct arithmetic reasoning. (Adapted from Kordemsky and Parry [1992])

In the Classroom (Ninth-Grade Students' Solutions)

Student 1: If x is the weight of the slab in pounds, then one side of the balance weighs x pounds and the other weighs

$$\frac{3}{4}x + \frac{3}{4},$$

so

$$x = \frac{3}{4}x + \frac{3}{4}.$$

Subtracting $\frac{3}{4}x$ from both sides gives

$$\frac{1}{4}x = \frac{3}{4},$$

so $x = 3$.

Student 2: It's just as easy without equations! If a slab of soap balances $\frac{3}{4}$ of a slab and $\frac{3}{4}$ pound, take $\frac{3}{4}$ of a slab off each side. That leaves $\frac{1}{4}$ of a slab on one side and $\frac{3}{4}$ pound on the other. So a quarter of a slab weighs $\frac{3}{4}$ of a pound. A full slab is four quarters, and that will make 3 pounds.

Teacher: Good! Can you see the connection between your two solutions?

Student 1: Oh, I see. What she did is really the same except she didn't use an x.

Key Mathematical Elements

Reasoning with Algebraic Symbols—Meaningful use of symbols; Reasoned solving

Reasoning Habits

Implementing a strategy—making purposeful use of procedures; making logical deductions
Seeking and using connections

Connecting Algebra with Geometry

An interplay exists between algebra and geometry: such geometric representations as graphs or figures can cast light on algebraic expressions and equations, and algebraic representations can be used to deduce geometric relationships (Katz 2007). Example 8 shows how the area model given in example 4, "A Model Idea," can be extended in a geometrically compelling way to help students make sense of completing the square, a process that students often find mysterious. This example additionally illustrates the power of an effective representation as a basis for reasoning and shows how structure can be uncovered in that representation to move toward a general solution.

Example 8: Squaring It Away

Task

Find a way of solving the equation $x^2 + 10x = 144$ by using an area model.

In the Classroom (Intermediate Algebra Class)

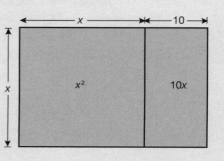

Teacher: Can anybody see how to think of $x^2 + 10x$ as an area?

Student 1: Well, x^2 is the area of a square with side x, and $10x$ is the area of a rectangle with sides x and 10, so we can put the rectangle and the square together like this. [See the figure at the right.] But I don't see how this helps.

Student 2: Maybe if we knew what the area of the square was, we could just take the square root to find x.

Teacher: Is there a way of rearranging the figure so that it's close to being a square?

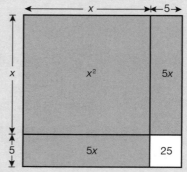

Student 1: I know! If we cut the rectangle into two rectangles of width 5, we could put one on each side like this! [See the figure at the right.]

Student 2: But it's not a complete square, it's missing a corner.

Teacher: What's the area of the corner?

Student 2: Oh, it must be 25, since the white square lines up with ends of the rectangles, so it has side length 5. And since the gray area is 144, the entire area of the big square is $144 + 25 = 169$.

Student 1: And that means the side length of the square is 13, so $x + 5 = 13$, which means $x = 8$.

Student 2: Shouldn't there be another solution, since the $(x + 5)$ is squared?

Example 8: Squaring It Away—*Continued*

Teacher:　Interesting point. Let's take a closer look. Can you write down what you did algebraically?

Student 2:　We started with $x^2 + 10x = 144$, and then we added 25 to the 144. I guess that means we add 25 to both sides of the equation, so we get $x^2 + 10x + 25 = 169$.

Student 1:　So to get 25, we divide the 10 by 2 to get 5, then square that to get 25.

Student 2:　Yeah, and then the left-hand side is a perfect square, so you get $(x + 5)^2 = 169$.

Student 1:　The algebraic way gives you both solutions, because you get $x + 5 = 13$ or $x + 5 = -13$, so $x = 8$ or $x = -18$, but I guess the area model can't give you the negative solution.

Teacher:　Good observations. The process of adding a constant to a quadratic expression so that it becomes a perfect square is called "completing the square." In the geometric interpretation, you just found that constant by adding in a corner piece. Can you see how this process might work for other quadratic equations?

The teacher could continue this discussion to lead to the development of the quadratic formula.

Key Mathematical Elements

Reasoning with Algebraic Symbols—Meaningful use of symbols; Mindful manipulation; Connecting algebra with geometry

Reasoning Habits

Analyzing a problem—looking for hidden structure
Seeking and using connections
Reflecting on a solution—revisiting initial assumptions; generalizing a solution

Linking Expressions and Functions

Although multiple representations of functions—symbolic, graphical, numerical, and verbal—are commonly seen, the idea of multiple *algebraic* representations of functions is less commonly made explicit. Different but equivalent ways of writing the same function may reveal different properties of the function, as illustrated in example 5, "Horseshoes in Flight."

Symbolic representation shifts to a higher level when we start to use letters to stand for functions and introduce function notation (Saul 2001). The magnitude of this shift is often overlooked. High school students have difficulty with extending the four basic arithmetic operations to functions and also with composition of functions. Embedding these experiences in a context may enhance students' comprehension of the concepts and improve both their retention and their ability to make connections (Katz 2007), as in example 5, "Horseshoes in Flight." Example 9 illustrates the power of using technology to link functions and expressions in an abstract mathematical context.

Building fluency in working with algebraic notation that is grounded in reasoning and sense making will ensure that students can flexibly apply the powerful tools of algebra in a variety of contexts both within and outside mathematics.

Example 9: More Than Meets the Eye

Task

In earlier grades you may have seen problems that asked you to find the next term in a sequence, such as 3, 7, 11. One possible answer is 15, assuming the sequence is generated by evaluating $f(x) = 4x - 1$ at $x = 1, 2, 3$. But are other answers possible?

In the Classroom (Fourth-Year Mathematics)

Teacher: Find the sequence generated by evaluating $g(x) = x^3 - 6x^2 + 15x - 7$ at $x = 1, 2, 3$.

Student: I get $g(1) = 3$, $g(2) = 7$, and $g(3) = 11$. It's the same sequence: 3, 7, 11.

Teacher: What would be the next term if you used $g(x)$ instead of $f(x)$?

Student: It would be $g(4) = 21$. That's different from what we get by using $f(x)$.

Teacher: Can you find other polynomials that generate the sequence 3, 7, 11?

Student: I don't see how you came up with that weird cubic for g in the first place.

Teacher: What does it mean when we say that $g(1) = 3$?

Student: Well, it means that the y-value, or output, is 3 when the x-value, or input, is 1.

Teacher: So how can two different functions, f and g, have the same values at $x = 1, 2$, and 3?

Student: I suppose that both of their graphs would have to have the same y-values.... Hey, that means they must intersect at those three points! Let me check that by graphing them. Yes, when I graph them, I see that the straight line graph of $f(x)$ intersects the cubic graph of $g(x)$ at $x = 1, 2$, and 3.

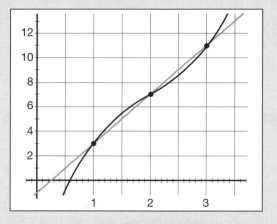

Teacher: Can you see now how you might find another polynomial graphically?

Student: Maybe I could figure out a way to change the shape of the cubic graph but keep the intersection points the same.

Teacher: How would you do that algebraically?

Student: I could try to stretch the difference between $f(x)$ and $g(x)$, which is $g(x) - f(x) = x^3 - 6x^2 + 11x - 6$. I could triple that, for example, and add it back on to $f(x)$ and get $4x - 1 + 3(x^3 - 6x^2 + 11x - 6) = 3x^3 - 18x^2 + 37x - 19$.

Example 9: More Than Meets the Eye—*Continued*

Teacher: Excellent. Now I want to understand what is really going on here. Is there anything special about the polynomial $x^3 - 6x^2 + 11x - 6$ that makes this work?

Student: Not that I can see.

Teacher: Why don't you try factoring it on your CAS?

▪ `f(x)=4x-1`	`f(x)=4·x-1`
▪ `g(x)=x^3-6x^2+15x-7`	`g(x)=x³-6·x²+15·x-7`
▪ `h(x)=g(x)-f(x)`	`h(x)=x³-6·x²+11·x-6`
▪ `factor(h(x))`	`(x-3)·(x-2)·(x-1)`
▪ `j(x)=f(x)+3*h(x)`	`j(x)=3·x³-18·x²+37·x-19`
▪ `j(1)`	`3`
▪ `j(2)`	`7`
▪ `j(3)`	`11`
▪	

Student: I get $x^3 - 6x^2 + 11x - 6 = (x - 1)(x - 2)(x - 3)$. Oh, I see. When I look at the factored form, I can see that the difference between $f(x)$ and $g(x)$ is 0 at $x = 1, 2,$ and 3. So I could get many polynomials that generate the same sequence just by adding a multiple of this polynomial to $f(x)$.

Teacher: What is the general form of such a polynomial?

Student: It is $4x - 1 + k(x - 1) \cdot (x - 2)(x - 3)$, where k can be any real number. When I look at my graphing program, I notice that as k increases, the graph of the polynomial stretches away from the line.

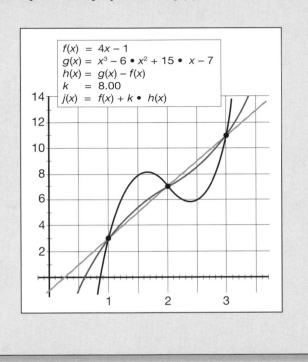

Example 9: More Than Meets the Eye—*Continued*

Key Mathematical Elements

Reasoning with Algebraic Symbols—Mindful manipulation; Linking expressions and functions

Reasoning with Functions—Using multiple representations of functions

Reasoning Habits

Analyzing a problem—identifying relevant concepts, representations, or procedures; seeking patterns and relationships

Seeking and using connections

Chapter 6

Reasoning with Functions

FUNCTIONS are one of the most important mathematical tools for helping students make sense of the world around them, as well as preparing them for further study in mathematics (Yerushalmy and Shternberg 2001). Functions appear in most branches of mathematics and provide a consistent way of making connections between and among topics. Students' continuing development of the concept of function must be rooted in reasoning, and likewise functions are an important tool for reasoning. Thus, developing procedural fluency in using functions is a significant goal of high school mathematics.

Key elements of reasoning and sense making with functions include the following:

- *Using multiple representations of functions.* Representing functions in various ways, including tabular, graphic, symbolic (explicit and recursive), visual, and verbal; making decisions about which representations are most helpful in problem-solving circumstances; and moving flexibly among those representations.

- *Modeling by using families of functions.* Working to develop a reasonable mathematical model for a particular contextual situation by applying knowledge of the characteristic behaviors of different families of functions.

- *Analyzing the effects of parameters.* Using a general representation of a function in a given family (e.g., the vertex form of a quadratic, $f(x) = a(x - h)^2 + k$) to analyze the effects of varying coefficients or other parameters; converting between different forms of functions (e.g., the standard form of a quadratic and its factored form) according to the requirements of the problem-solving situation (e.g., finding the vertex of a quadratic or finding its zeros).

We address these key elements in more detail in the following sections.

Using Multiple Representations of Functions

Different representations of a function—tables, graphs or diagrams, symbolic expressions, and verbal descriptions—exhibit different properties. Using a variety of representations can help make functions more understandable to a wider range of students than can be accomplished by working with symbolic representations alone (Lloyd and Wilson 1998; Coulombe and Berenson 2001). Students need to establish connections among different representations, for example, the relationship among the zeros of a function, the solution of an equation, and the *x*-intercepts of graphs.

Functions whose domains are the natural numbers are often represented recursively, where $f(k + 1)$ is defined in terms of $f(k)$ and an initial function value is given. Such functions can also be presented as sequences, and they are used in applications involving discrete rather than continuous data, often with the support of a calculator or an electronic spreadsheet; see example 10, "Patterns, Plane and Symbol," and example 11, "Take As Directed."

One interesting exploration is to investigate the number of regions into which a plane is divided by *n* straight lines. The first question is whether *n* lines always divide the plane into the same number of regions. Experiments with two or three lines should help students see that different numbers of regions result. For example, two lines that cross create four regions, whereas two parallel lines create only three. Three parallel lines produce four regions; three lines all going through the same point create six regions; but three nonparallel, nonconcurrent lines create seven regions. In general, *n* parallel lines create only *n* + 1 regions, whereas *n* lines that all pass through the same point create 2*n* regions. The next example explores what happens in the case of nonparallel, nonconcurrent lines. It could be used with students entering high school, who are beginning to develop the ability to express functional relationships symbolically, or with more advanced students who are working to improve their proficiency with algebraic manipulation. Example 10 illustrates how students can use various representations of functions, including verbal descriptions, tables, formulas, and various geometric models to make sense of a problem.

Example 10: Patterns, Plane and Symbol

Task

Develop a symbolic representation for a function that produces the number of regions in a plane formed by intersecting lines such that no two lines are parallel and no more than two lines intersect in the same point, as shown in the figure.

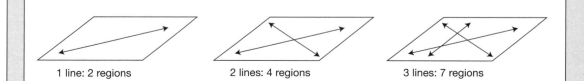

| 1 line: 2 regions | 2 lines: 4 regions | 3 lines: 7 regions |

In the Classroom

Students may approach this problem in several different ways, depending on their level of mathematical experience.

Method 1. After exploring a number of cases, possibly using an interactive geometry tool, students may produce a table of values for the number of lines, *L*, and the number of regions, *R*, as shown here:

No. of lines (*L*)	1	2	3	4	5	6
No. of regions (*R*)	2	4	7	11	16	22

Example 10: Patterns, Plane and Symbol—*Continued*

Students commonly observe the pattern of differences between consecutive terms of a sequence. This observation lends itself to a recursive definition of a function. In this example, a recursive definition would be $R(1) = 2$, $R(L) = R(L-1) + L$.

Method 2. An interesting geometric approach to helping students reason about this problem is to use checkers, coins, tiles, or other small objects to create a pattern in which the value of L defines the number of rows of objects and the value of R defines the total number of objects in the figure, as shown in the following sequence:

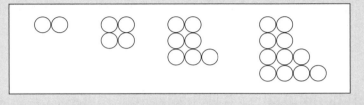

Removing one of the objects from the top row results in a triangular pattern, as shown below:

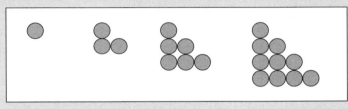

Doubling and transforming this pattern can result in a rectangle containing $L(L + 1)$ objects, as shown here:

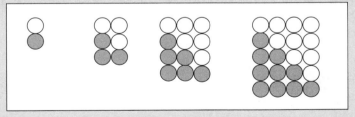

From this configuration, one can see that the original objects, minus the one that was removed, form half the rectangle. The explicit definition of this function can then be written as

$$R = \frac{1}{2}(L)(L+1) + 1 = \frac{1}{2}L^2 + \frac{1}{2}L + 1.$$

Example 10: Patterns, Plane and Symbol—*Continued*

This type of approach demonstrates how a student who is given the opportunity to represent a function pictorially can use a simple geometric pattern to write the explicit definition of the function. The student can then extend his or her reasoning about symbolic representations by developing it from a familiar starting place.

Method 3. By applying technology to numeric and graphical reasoning, students may enter a number of ordered pairs from the table into a graphing calculator and examine a scatterplot of the pairs to conjecture that the relationship is quadratic because of the parabolic shape of the graph. On the basis of that conjecture, students could use calculator-assisted quadratic regression to find the function $R = 0.5L^2 + 0.5L + 1$. This algebraic model could be tested by using ordered pairs from the table.

Method 4. The teacher could ask students to focus on the differences between consecutive terms of the sequence of R values: 2, 3, 4, 5, and so forth. By applying algebraic reasoning, students may examine the data and observe that the function is quadratic because the first differences are linear so the second differences are constant. The geometric representation shown in part 1 of this example can be used to reinforce this concept for students. Writing a system of equations of the form $R = aL^2 + bL + c$, substituting three ordered pairs, and solving the system would reveal that

$$a = \frac{1}{2}, \ b = \frac{1}{2}, \ \text{and} \ c = 1; \ \text{thus}$$

$$R = \frac{1}{2}L^2 + \frac{1}{2}L + 1.$$

This strategy would require a sophisticated understanding of several mathematical topics and a command of algebraic manipulation developed later in the high school experience.

Key Elements of Mathematics

Reasoning with Functions—Using multiple representations of functions
Reasoning with Algebraic Symbols—Connecting algebra with geometry; Linking expressions and functions

Reasoning Habits

Analyzing a problem—seeking patterns and relationships
Seeking and using connections
Reflecting on a solution—justifying or validating a solution

Modeling by Using Families of Functions

According to *Curriculum Focal Points* (NCTM 2006a), students should enter high school having had extensive experience with linear functions and some exposure to nonlinear functions. High school experiences can help students build on this knowledge and work with parameterized families of functions (e.g., linear, quadratic, exponential, and periodic), each of which has distinguishing characteristics common to all members of the family. Given data from a problem situation, students should be able to (a) choose a family of functions that sensibly models the situation; (b) find parameters for a function to approximately match the data; (c) use the resulting function to solve the problem; and (d) interpret and reflect on their solution in the context of the problem.

Using problems that can be extended and revisited as students mature is a powerful way to help students make connections between existing knowledge and new learning. Example 11 uses a context to which students can readily relate and demonstrates how a problem can be extended as students' mathematical backgrounds become more sophisticated. It also shows the power of deductive reasoning in developing a general solution to a problem.

Example 11: Take As Directed

Task

A student strained her knee in an intramural volleyball game, and her doctor has prescribed an anti-inflammatory drug to reduce the swelling. The student takes two 220 mg tablets every 8 hours for 10 days. Her kidneys eliminate 60 percent of this drug from her body every 8 hours. Determine how much of the drug is in her system after 10 days, just after she takes her last dose of medicine. Explain what happens to the change in the amount of medicine in the body as time progresses and why this pattern occurs. If she continued to take the drug for a year, how much of the drug would be in her system just after she took her last dose? Explain, in mathematical terms and in terms of body metabolism, why the long-term amount of medicine in the body is reasonable (adapted from NCTM [2000b]).

In the Classroom (Variety of Levels from First-Year to Fourth-Year Mathematics)

Students may examine this problem in varying degrees of depth, depending on their level of mathematical experience:

Method 1. Students who are near the beginning of their high school experience could produce a table of data and generate a discrete graph of the data. The following table and graph show the amount of medicine, A_n, in mg, in the athlete's body just after taking n doses of medicine.

n	1	2	3	4	5	6	7	8
A_n	440	616	686.40	714.56	725.82	730.33	732.13	732.85

n	9	10	11	12	...	20	...	30
A_n	733.14	733.26	733.30	733.32	...	733.33	...	733.33

Example 11: Take As Directed—*Continued*

Students may observe that the level of medicine in the body initially rises rapidly but with time increases less rapidly. Thus, the rate of change of this function does not remain constant. Even a beginning student could surmise from this table that the medicine level appears to eventually stabilize, so that after about seventeen dosage periods, the value no longer seems to change. In terms of metabolism, students could explain that the athlete's body is eliminating the same amount of medication as she is taking in each dose. This observation can be mathematically verified by showing that

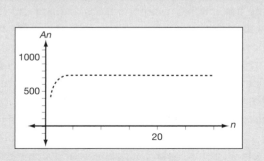

$$0.6\left(733\tfrac{1}{3}\right) = 440$$

because the value of A_n approaches a limiting value of

$$733\tfrac{1}{3} \text{ mg}$$

after about seventeen doses.

Method 2. A problem such as this can be expressed in recursive notation. A recursive definition for the sequence of medicine levels in the athlete's body would be $A_{n+1} = 0.40A_n + 440$, $A_1 = 0$. Obtaining explicit formulas from tables of data is often quite difficult and in some situations, impossible. A recursive approach, especially when supported by a calculator or an electronic spreadsheet, is more intuitive and gives students access to such interesting problems as this earlier in their schooling.

Method 3. Students who are studying exponential functions might use a problem such as this to develop their understanding of exponential decay. By examining the pattern of medicine levels, students can observe that the change of medicine level in the athlete's body is decreasing; specifically, each change is 40 percent of the previous amount of change. After reasoning about the repetitive nature of multiplying by 0.4, students could express this relationship with the explicit function

$$I(n) = 440(0.4^{n-1}),$$

where $I(n)$ represents the increase in medicine level after dose number n. When students are ready, an illuminating exercise would be to verify this result formally, as follows:

If a sequence A_n satisfies a linear recursion $A_{n+1} = a \cdot A_n + b$ for some constants a and b, then the differences $A_{n+1} - A_n$ satisfy the simpler recursion

Example 11: Take As Directed—*Continued*

$$A_{n+1} - A_n = (a \cdot A_n + b) - (a \cdot A_{n-1} + b) = a \cdot (A_n - A_{n-1}).$$

Therefore, these differences are just powers of a times the first difference:

$$A_{n+1} - A_n = a^n (A_1 - A_0).$$

Note that we can show from this result that A_n itself is the sum of a geometric progression. Thus, this kind of problem can provide another motivation for an application of geometric progressions.

Method 4. For older students with a more sophisticated mathematical background, this problem could be revisited as a means of informally introducing them to the important mathematical concept of limit, especially when coupled with a discrete graph of the sequence, as shown in the graph on the previous page.

Method 5. Students who have more experience with reasoning and sense making may be asked to formally justify why the level of medicine converges, thus creating a deeper understanding of the phenomenon and why it happens. In this approach to the problem, students are asked to use a formal proof to show that the sequence will converge for large numbers of doses. For instance, consider the recursive function for the amount A of medicine in the athlete's body after n doses:

(1) $$A_{n+1} = A_n - 0.6A_n + 440 = 0.4A_n + 440.$$

We can define the behavior of the medicine level as a linear function C, called the *transition function governing the sequence A_n*, where

(2) $$C(x) = 0.4x + 440.$$

By substitution, we can write

(3) $$A_{n+1} = 0.4A_n + 440 = C(A_n).$$

Now if the medicine concentrations truly level off, we can let V represent the fixed value approached by A_n after a certain number of doses, called the *fixed point of C*. Doing so leads to the equation

(4) $$C(V) = V, \text{ or } 0.4V + 440 = V.$$

Solving equation (4) for V gives us the value

$$V = 733\tfrac{1}{3},$$

which proves that the limiting value of the blood concentration is

Example 11: Take As Directed—*Continued*

$$V = 733\tfrac{1}{3} \text{ mg}$$

as explained by the transition function C, defined in equation (2).

To see how the transition function guarantees the convergence, we can rewrite it to display the difference between the actual amount and the fixed value. Define D_n as the difference between the actual amount of medicine, A_n, and the fixed value, V:

(5)
$$A_n = V + D_n.$$

Substituting this result in the recursion relation, equation (3), gives

(6)
$$A_{n+1} = 0.4(V + D_n) + 440 = (0.4V + 440) + 0.4D_n.$$

Since $A_{n+1} = V + D_{n+1}$, from equation (5), and since V is defined by the relation $V = 0.4V + 440$, from equation (4), we can reduce the relationship further:

$$V + D_{n+1} = (0.4V + 440) + 0.4D_n,$$
$$(0.4V + 440) + D_{n+1} = (0.4V + 440) + 0.4D_n.$$

From this result we can derive the simple recursion

(7)
$$D_{n+1} = 0.4D_n,$$

which shows that at each step, D_n shrinks to 40 percent of its previous value. Clearly, after not too many steps, D_n will become negligibly small, as was suggested by the foregoing numerical calculations.

Key Mathematical Elements

Reasoning with Functions—Using multiple representations of functions; Modeling by using families of functions

Reasoning with Algebraic Symbols—Meaningful use of symbols; Mindful manipulation

Reasoning Habits

Analyzing a problem—identifying relevant concepts, procedures, or representations; seeking patterns and relationships

Implementing a strategy—making logical deductions

Reflecting on a solution—justifying or validating a solution

Incorporating formal proof throughout the high school mathematics curriculum serves to strengthen students' reasoning skills and can also ease the transition from high school to college mathematics. The general reasoning in example 11, "Take As Directed," can be extended to a range of other situations, as shown in example 12, which demonstrates an application of formal proof to the important context of finance. This example shows how students can grow in their own reasoning ability by studying and interpreting the reasoning of others.

Example 12: Money Matters

Task

After exploring the method of formal justification in example 11 (method 5), a teacher asks her students to read and interpret the following text describing how to determine the payment amount for installment loans, and to answer a series of questions about the text.

When someone takes out an installment loan, we need to be able to find the monthly payment amount so that the loan is paid off in a certain number of months. The monthly payment on an installment loan includes the interest charged on the unpaid amount of the loan (the principal) since the last payment. Any amount of the payment left over after the interest is deducted goes toward paying off the loan, thereby reducing the principal.

Let's express this situation by using algebraic notation. Define P_n to be the principal owed at the end of period n, where P_0 is the amount initially borrowed. If the interest rate for a single period is r and the borrower makes a monthly payment M at the end of each period, then the principal owed at the end of the period $n + 1$ can be written as $P_{n+1} = P_n + rP_n - M = (1 + r)P_n - M$. Thus, the principal owed at the end of one month is related to the principal owed the month before by the linear function $P_{n+1} = Q(P_n)$, where $Q(x) = (1 + r)x - M$.

If we want to pay the principal off in m months, then $P_m = 0$. Noting that $P_m = Q(P_{m-1}) = Q(Q(P_{m-2})) = Q(Q(Q(P_{m-3})))$, and so forth, we can see that $P_m = Q^{(m)}(P_0) = 0$, where we use $Q^{(m)}$ to stand for the composition of Q with itself m times. If we can find an expression for $Q^{(m)}(P_0)$ in terms of P_0, M, m, and r, we can solve the equation $Q^{(m)}(P_0) = 0$ for M in terms of the given variables.

However, finding the expression is not easy. We can use a fixed-point analysis to simplify the effect of Q. If F is the fixed point of Q, then $Q(F) = F$. Thus, $Q(F) = (1 + r)F - M = F$. So we can see that $F = M/r$.

Next, let us define D_n as the difference between P_n and the fixed point F, that is,

$$D_n = P_n - F, \text{ or } P_n = F + D_n.$$

Then, on the one hand,

$$\begin{aligned} Q(P_n) &= Q(F + D_n) && \text{(from our definition of } D_n\text{)} \\ &= (1 + r)(F + D_n) - M && \text{(by applying the definition of } Q\text{)} \end{aligned}$$

(Continued)

Example 12: Money Matters—*Continued*

$$= ((1 + r)F - M) + (1 + r)D_n \qquad \text{(by distribution and rearranging terms)}$$

$$= Q(F) + (1 + r)D_n \qquad \text{(again by applying the definition of } Q \text{)}$$

$$= F + (1 + r)D_n \qquad \text{(since } F \text{ is the fixed point for } Q \text{)}.$$

On the other hand,

$$Q(P_n) = P_{n+1} \qquad \text{(by definition of } Q \text{)}$$

$$= F + D_{n+1} \qquad \text{(by definition of } D_{n+1} \text{)}.$$

Equating the two expressions for $Q(P_n)$ gives

$$F + (1 + r)D_n = F + D_{n+1} \qquad \text{or}$$

$$D_{n+1} = (1 + r)D_n.$$

Thus, D_n, the difference between P_n and the fixed point F, varies in a simpler way than P_n does: it is simply multiplied by $(1 + r)$ at each step.

Applying this relation twice gives

$$D_{n+2} = (1 + r)D_{n+1} \qquad \text{(by substituting } n + 1 \text{ for } n \text{)}$$

$$= (1 + r)((1 + r)D_n) \qquad \text{(by the equation for } n \text{)}$$

$$= (1 + r)^2 D_n \qquad \text{(by the associative rule and the definition of exponents)}.$$

Iterating this reasoning gives us the relation

$$D_m = (1 + r)^m D_0.$$

If we rewrite this result in terms of P_m, we find

$$P_m = F + D_m = F + (1 + r)^m D_0 = F + (1 + r)^m (P_0 - F)$$

$$= (1 + r)^m P_0 + F(1 - (1 + r)^m).$$

By using the formula $F = M/r$, we get

$$P_m = (1 + r)^m P_0 + (M/r)(1 - (1 + r)^m),$$

which is the expression we were looking for. By setting $P_m = 0$, we can now solve for M:

$$M = r \cdot P_0 \cdot \frac{(1+r)^m}{(1+r)^m - 1}.$$

Example 12: Money Matters—*Continued*

Answer the following questions about this analysis:

1. How does the function describing the successive periods of an installment loan compare with the function describing the blood concentrations in successive periods when taking a medicine?

2. Compare the effect of Q in this situation and C in the medicine problem, example 11. Why do we want to find a fixed point in each situation?

3. How does the multiplier $(1 + r)$ differ between this situation and the medicine problem, example 11? How does the value of the multiplier ensure that we can eventually pay off the loan?

4. Explain how the underlying mathematics in this situation is very similar to finding the blood concentration of medicine, even though the two situations appear very different.

Key Mathematical Elements

Reasoning with Functions—Modeling by using families of functions
Reasoning with Algebraic Symbols—Mindful manipulation; Reasoned solving

Reasoning Habits

Analyzing a problem—defining relevant variables and conditions
Implementing a strategy—making logical deductions
Reflecting on a solution—reconciling different approaches; generalizing a solution

Analyzing the Effects of Parameters

Different but equivalent algebraic expressions can be used to define the same function, often revealing different properties of the function. For example, writing a quadratic function in the form $y = ax^2 + bx + c$ helps us identify the y-axis intercept, whereas using the form

$$y = \left(\frac{1}{4p}\right)(x - h)^2 + k$$

enables us to quickly determine the vertex, (h, k), of the parabolic graph and the location of its focus, where p represents the distance from the vertex to the focus. In example 13, students make conjectures about the effects of changes to the values of parameters in a sinusoidal function and consider the reasonableness of their solution.

Example 13: Tidal Waves

Task

The captain of a shipping vessel must consider the tides when entering a seaport because the water depth can vary greatly from one time of day to another. Suppose that high tide in a certain port occurs at 5:00 a.m., when the water is 10.6 meters deep, and the next low tide occurs at 11:00 a.m., when the water is 6.5 meters deep. Develop a mathematical model that will predict the water depth as a function of the elapsed time since midnight.

In the Classroom (Fourth-Year Mathematics)

Note that the students working on this problem have had experience with transformations of linear and quadratic functions and are familiar with the graphs of the sine and cosine functions.

An example of students' reasoning about this task follows:

Teacher: We have only been given two ordered pairs, so there are many types of graphs that could fit our data. What type of algebraic model would make sense in this situation?

Student 1:   Two points determine a line, right? Couldn't we just connect the two points?

Student 2:   No, the water level doesn't just keep going down forever—it goes back up again and then down again every day.

Student 3:   That means it's probably going to be one of those wave-shaped graphs.

Student 1:   Oh, yeah—I'll bet it's going to be sine or cosine. But how do we know which one?

Student 3:   Well, let's try drawing part of the wave and see what we can figure out.

Student 2:   If the pattern repeats like this every six hours, then there will be two high points and two low points every day. I suppose that makes the period 12 hours.

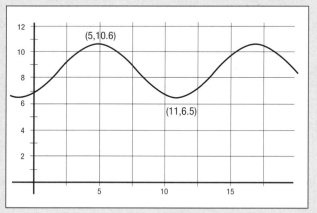

Student 3:   Yeah, and if the highest and lowest the graph ever goes are 10.6 meters and 6.5 meters, then the amplitude is going to be 4.1 meters, right? Oh, wait a minute—the amplitude is only half of the height, so we need to change that to 2.05 meters.

Example 13: Tidal Waves—*Continued*

Student 2:   OK, now once we know that, we can find out that the vertical shift is half-way between the high and low points, which would make it 8.55 meters.

Teacher: Good job so far—now you just need to work on the period and horizontal shift. Do you think it would be easier to work with sine or cosine?

Student 1:   I like cosine better for this graph because we can see that a high point happens five hours after midnight, so that will make it easy to find the horizontal shift.

The conversation could continue like this in small groups, followed by a whole-class discussion of the observations made by various groups. Students could check the reasonableness of their solutions by using a dynamic graphing utility. An interesting extension of this task would be to use the model to determine the times during which a ship with a certain depth requirement would be able to safely navigate into and out of the port.

Key Elements of Mathematics

Reasoning with Functions—Modeling by using families of functions; Analyzing the effects of parameters

Reasoning Habits

Analyzing a problem—applying previously learned concepts; making preliminary deductions and conjectures
Reflecting on a solution—considering the reasonableness of a solution

Opportunities to reason with functions and use them to model real-world situations arise at every stage of a high school student's mathematical development. Providing students with varied experiences involving functions can help them internalize the sometimes confusing mathematical language of function notation (Chazan and Yerushalmy 2003; Coulombe and Berenson 2001). The development of reasoning with functions is one of the cornerstones on which a well-developed understanding of mathematics is built.

Chapter 7

Reasoning with Geometry

CLASSICALLY, geometry has been the subject in which students encounter mathematical proof based on formal deduction. Although proof should be naturally incorporated in all areas of the curriculum, attention to proof in the geometry curriculum is strengthened by a focus on reasoning and sense making. In addition, geometry has connections with other mathematical domains and important applications in careers and in everyday life. Geometric ideas are a significant part of many high-technology developments, including high-definition television (HDTV), global positioning systems (GPS), computer animation, computerized axial tomography (CAT) scans, cellular telephone networks, robotics, virtual reality, and docking of the Space Shuttle. Geometric and visual reasoning often enter our daily lives.

A considerable amount of research on students' thinking in geometry can be used to promote students' reasoning and sense making in this area. Much of this research bolsters the van Hiele levels of students' geometric thinking (Battista 2007). These five van Hiele levels of thinking are sequential and hierarchical, meaning that students must pass through lower levels if they are to attain higher levels. The van Hiele levels of students' thinking can be linked to the reasoning habits described in chapter 2 and can help promote students' attainment of the reasoning and sense-making abilities exemplified in this publication. For instance, the first two van Hiele levels, *visual-holistic* and *descriptive-analytic* reasoning, link to the *empirical* reasoning level described in "Progression of Reasoning" in chapter 2. The third van Hiele level, *relational-inferential* reasoning, connects with the *preformal* level, and the fourth and fifth van Hiele levels, *formal deductive proof* and *rigor*, are tied to the *formal* level of reasoning. Accordingly, knowledge about students' thinking not only allows us but requires us to support students at whatever level of thinking they may have attained when coming to high school and to provide them experiences that help them move to higher levels.

Key elements of reasoning and sense making with geometry include the following:

- *Conjecturing about geometric objects.* Analyzing configurations and reasoning inductively about relationships to formulate conjectures.

- *Construction and evaluation of geometric arguments.* Developing and evaluating deductive arguments (both formal and informal) about figures and their properties that help make sense of geometric situations.

- *Multiple geometric approaches.* Analyzing mathematical situations by using transformations, synthetic approaches, and coordinate systems.

- *Geometric connections and modeling.* Using geometric ideas, including spatial visualization, in other areas of mathematics, other disciplines, and in real-world situations.

We address these key elements in more detail in the following sections.

Conjecturing about Geometric Objects

Making conjectures is a fundamental reasoning habit in mathematical inquiry. Geometry offers many opportunities for developing this reasoning habit through an abundance of intriguing and often surprising visual or measurable geometric relationships. Students can make conjectures by analyzing a planar or spatial configuration or by wondering whether a certain configuration can exist. Conjecturing activates their natural inquisitiveness, not only about "what might be happening" (the conjecture) but "why it would be happening" (looking for insight, validation, or refutation.) The process of seeking and making conjectures gives students the opportunity to become immersed in, and deepen their understanding of, the mathematical relationships involved, as well to sharpen their ability to validate them. By making conjectures about novel situations, students also learn to employ mathematics in new situations, a highly desirable skill in our fast-changing world. Further mention of this skill is made in the section titled "Geometric connections and modeling."

In example 14 students develop mathematical conjectures related to a context drawn from everyday life. In addition to the immediate utility of the results in the context itself, such contexts (1) provide a recognizable, interesting situation in which students can immerse themselves for the purpose of mathematical analysis, (2) offer multiple accessible methods to explore the situation for the purpose of creating conjectures, and (3) foster the notion that mathematics is everywhere. Example 15, "Circling the Points," builds on example 14. These two examples would appear in the curriculum after students have studied some properties of perpendicularity (e.g., that a point lies on the perpendicular bisector of a line segment if and only if it is equidistant from the two endpoints of the segment.) They would appear early in the study of geometric properties of circles and would ultimately lead to the study of the inscribed angle theorem and related results. These examples also support the reasoning habits of making conjectures and using deduction to explore those conjectures.

Example 14: Picture This

Task

In photography, the "horizontal viewing angle" describes the angular extent of a scene being captured, with the vertex representing the camera lens. (See the figure at the right, which depicts the horizontal plane of the camera shot.)

Shelly wants to take an artistic photo of the decorated side of a building that sits on a flat plot of land. She wants to capture a level shot of the full width of the building (exactly), but she does not care whether the full building height is in the picture. So the horizontal expanse of the picture is fixed.

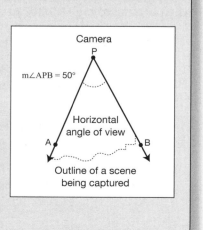

Example 14: Picture This—*Continued*

She is using a camera lens with a fixed horizontal viewing angle of 50 degrees, and she wants to take a level shot of the side of the building. She has found one spot that works, as indicated by point *P* in the figure at the right. Shelly believes that she could stand at other places to capture the same horizontal expanse but from a different perspective. Before she snaps the picture, she wants to examine some of those other positions. Your task is to figure out the ground locations where Shelly could stand to create a picture fitting her criteria.

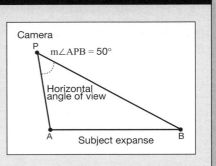

Explore the situation, write down any conjectures you have regarding possible positions, and justify any that you can. The objective is to eventually create a conjecture describing the full range of possible positions. Prepare to clearly state your conjectures, as well as the thinking, exploration, and reasoning that explain how you arrived at them.

In the Classroom (Geometry Class)

An interactive drawing utility (with a file containing the sketch above), a hard copy of the sketch and a physical manipulative (a rigid angle—e.g., the expanse of a rigid compass), or a real camera and wall could be used to facilitate exploration of possible locations. The lesson begins with a full-class discussion of initial thoughts. After some time for individual thought or explanation, the following dialogue ensues.

Teacher: Do you have any immediate conjectures to suggest?

Student 1:   I think there is a point right in the middle where you could stand.

Teacher: What do you mean by "middle"?

Student 1:   I mean I would stand at a point in the diagram that would be the same distance from points *A* and *B*.

Student 2:   Oh, that means the point would be somewhere on the perpendicular bisector of the segment *AB,* which represents the building side. This is because we have already learned that the perpendicular bisector of the segment is the collection of points that are equidistant from points *A* and *B*.

Teacher: How would you find such a point?

The students engage in some more work.

Student 1:   I'd put a point on the perpendicular bisector of segment *AB* and then move it back and forth until the angle exactly fit the segment.

Teacher: Good, that gives some detail regarding how one might locate a second point. [The teacher writes down a conjecture that there is a possible vertex location on the perpendicular bisector of segment *AB*. This conjecture will be addressed in a subsequent discussion—beyond the confines of this example.] Are there other ideas about possible vertices?

Example 14: Picture This—*Continued*

Student 2:   Based on my experience with a camera, I think there would be many points where one could stand to show the entire building side.

Many students in the class agree with the conjecture that many points would work. Another student jumps in and suggests that that the possible positions possess symmetry. Eventually, someone states that reflective symmetry would be evident in the collection of possible points across the perpendicular bisector of *AB*. This conjecture will be evaluated subsequently, as well.

Teacher: Now, by using either the interactive drawing utility or the physical manipulative, plot a collection of points that represent where the photographer might stand to snap the required image. See if any other conjectures emerge from this exploration.

Student 4:   [After some exploration] All the points seem to be on a circular arc that goes from point *A* to point *B*—even though the photographer can't stand there.

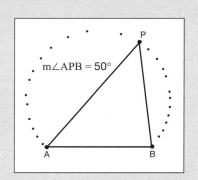

The teacher next facilitates a discussion about stating in abstract terms what we refer to as the major conjecture: "Given a line segment *AB* and a specified side of line *AB*, each point, *P*, on the specified side of *AB* with the property that *m∠APB* = 50° lies on a circular arc containing *A* and *B*."

This conjecture is not resolved immediately. Rather, a set of questions is compiled by the class for moving toward a proof of this conjecture. These questions include the following:

1. Can we find out which circular arc we are talking about? That is, can we find the circle that contains this arc?

2. Would every point on the arc (except points *A* and *B*) represent possible positions where the photographer could stand?

3. Would the arc miss any possible points?

(See example 15 along with the supporting topic book on geometry for a full discussion of the conjecture.)

Key Elements of Mathematics

Reasoning with Geometry—Conjecturing about geometric objects; Multiple geometric approaches

Reasoning Habits

Analyzing the problem—identifying relevant concepts, representations, or procedures; looking for hidden structure; considering special cases or simpler analogs; seeking patterns and relationships; making preliminary deductions and conjectures

Implementing a strategy—monitoring progress toward a solution; making logical deductions

Construction and Evaluation of Geometric Arguments

Making a conjecture, as in example 14, is a first step in mathematical inquiry. Students need to follow up many of their conjectures with efforts to either justify or disprove them. Although the major conjecture in example 14 is not resolved immediately, the activity leads naturally to the development of several important geometric results that emerge from question 1 in the example. In particular, the students in example 15 make progress toward resolving the conjecture by establishing the fact that three noncollinear points in the plane lie on a unique circle. Further progress is made when students prove the inscribed angle theorem, which states that every point, P, on the conjectured circular arc would satisfy the condition that $m\angle APB$ equals 50 degrees. However, students would still need to prove that no other point on the same side of line AB could be the vertex of such an angle. Example 15 also exemplifies the reasoning habit of looking for hidden structure—in this example, an auxiliary line.

The progress in levels of reasoning can clearly be seen in these two examples. Students begin with explorations at the empirical level, moving to the preformal level as students suggest initial conclusions that can be drawn, such as that the arc actually passes through endpoints A and B. Example 15 picks up the discussion with increasingly formal reasoning, culminating in conclusions supported by formal proof.

Example 15: Circle of Points

Task

This task answers question 1 raised at the end of example 14, "Picture This": What circle contains the conjectured arc?

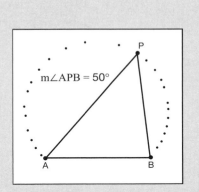

In the Classroom (Geometry Class)

Students are divided into groups with the assignment to decide what to do next. After a short time, the groups report on possible strategies:

Group 1: We think you need to find the center and radius of the circle.

Group 2: We think you just need to find the center of the circle. You don't need to find the radius, because you already know at least one point on the circle—either the point P specified in the original problem or points A or B, which are part of the conjecture. You can use the center and one of these points on the circle to draw the whole circle.

Group 3: We think you need the center. We think the center should be a point on segment AB halfway between A and B. The radius should be half the length of segment AB.

The groups reconvene to discuss these and possibly other thoughts. After a few more minutes the groups report.

Example 15: Circle of Points—*Continued*

Group 4:   We tested to see if the midpoint of segment *AB* would be the center. The circle did not go through the point *P* we were given, so the midpoint is not the center in this case. So next we used the interactive drawing utility to try to create the circle that fit the points and figure out its center. We got a pretty good circle. We didn't think it would fit all the points because we just approximated the locations of points that would be vertices of 50 degree angles when we made them. But we are even more convinced that there is a circle through the point *P*, which we were using for the 50 degree angle, and points *A* and *B*—and all actual real points where the photographer could stand.

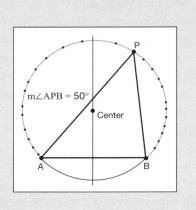

We then tried to think about the center and agreed that the center (like the midpoint of segment *AB*) needs to be equidistant from both *A* and *B*, since the circle goes through *A* and *B*. Thinking back to what we talked about when we started example 14, we conclude that the center of the circle has to be on the perpendicular bisector of segment *AB*. We added the perpendicular bisector of segment *AB* to our drawing, and it went right through the center of the circle we had drawn—just like it was supposed to!

Then someone else in our group noticed that the same reasoning works with the two points *A* and *P*. That is, since the circle goes through *A* and *P*, its center would have to lie on the perpendicular bisector of the segment *AP*, as well. We added the perpendicular bisector of segment *AP* to our sketch, constructed these two bisectors, and found that they intersect in one point, which we called *G*. That is the only point that lies on both perpendicular bisectors.

So it is the only possible point for the center of a circle. So we could now draw the circle by choosing the center and any one of the points *A, P,* or *B*.

Teacher: Before you draw your circle, let me ask you a question. It seems that you have shown that *if* there is a circle through the points *P, A,* and *B*, the center must be *G*. Can you or any other group prove that there will definitely be such a circle—that you weren't just lucky this time with these particular points or that the drawing is misleading? Let's work on that in our groups.

Example 15: Circle of Points—*Continued*

After a few minutes, a new group is ready to contribute its proof:

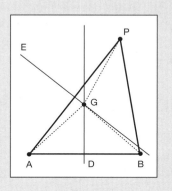

Group 5: We are assuming that we have the three noncollinear points *P*, *A*, and *B* and that *G* is the point of intersection of the perpendicular bisectors of sides *AB* and *AP*—like we have been talking about. We will show that *G is* the center of a circle that goes through points *P*, *A*, and *B*. Construct segments *GP*, *GA*, and *GB*. Segments *GP* and *GA* have to have equal lengths because *G* is on the perpendicular bisector of segment *AP*. Segments *GA* and *GB* must be equal in length because *G* is on the perpendicular bisector of segment *AB*. Since both segments *GP* and *GB* are equal in length to segment *GA*, all three segments have equal length. So if we draw the circle with center *G* and radius equal to the length of segment *GA*, the circle will definitely go through the three points *A*, *B*, and *P*.

The teacher asks for comments and critiques from the class with regard to group 5's presentation. (There are none.) The teacher then proposes that the day's discussion suggests three results: (1) Three noncollinear points in the plane determine a unique circle. (2) (Circle construction algorithm) The center of that circle can be found by finding the point of intersection of the perpendicular bisectors of any two sides of the triangle that has the three noncollinear points as vertices. (3) The perpendicular bisectors of the three sides of a triangle intersect in a single point. The first two of these results comes directly from the discussion. The third is closely related.

For homework, students are asked to write proofs of the first and third statements. In some instances this assignment requires organization, generalization, or extension of arguments given in the discussion. In others it involves adding detail. For the second statement, the students are asked to write an algorithm (i.e., well-defined sequence of steps) for constructing a circle through three noncollinear points in the plane.

Key Elements

Reasoning with Geometry—Construction and evaluation of geometric arguments

Reasoning Habits

Analyzing a problem—identifying relevant mathematical concepts, representations, or procedures; looking for hidden structure

Implementing a strategy—organizing a solution; making logical deductions; monitoring progress toward a solution

Reflecting on a solution—justifying or validating a solution

The validity of a proof is not determined by how it is presented. A two-column proof is not necessarily more valid (or rigorous) than a proof given in paragraph form. In fact, strict adherence to a specific proof format may elevate focus on form over function, thus obstructing the creative mix of reasoning habits and ultimately hindering the chance of students' successfully understanding the mathematical consequences of the arguments (Herbst 2002). In addition to facility in constructing chains of reasoning, constructing a mathematical proof often requires resourcefulness in selecting a strategy, cultured intuition, and good judgment. Blind alleys and false starts sometimes generate insight along with the inevitable frustration that accompanies them—therein lies the challenge!

Multiple Geometric Approaches

Geometric situations can be approached in many different ways, including the synthetic approach seen in examples 14 and 15 and the coordinate approach seen in the example involving the distance formula in chapter 1. The coordinate approach applies algebraic concepts in geometric contexts, and vice versa.

The value of transformations in geometry has been recognized for more than thirty years (cf. Coxford and Usiskin [1971]; NCTM [1989, 2000a]), although they continue to receive limited attention in many curricula. Geometric transformations—rotations, translations, reflections, and dilations—provide another useful approach to understanding geometric relationships. The transformation approach to geometry supports an alternative way of considering congruence, similarity, and symmetry. In example 16, students are challenged to go beyond simple but misleading rules and think carefully about rotational symmetry. Example 16 also exemplifies the reasoning habit of monitoring one's progress, including considering approaches taken by other members of the class.

Example 16: Taking a Spin

Task

What regular polygons have 80-degree rotational symmetry?

In the Classroom (Geometry Class)

Students have been asked to answer the following problem for homework: "What regular polygons have 80-degree rotational symmetry?" (Martin 1996). At the beginning of class the following day, class members discuss this problem in small groups. One group goes to the front of the class to present its solution.

Student 1:   We concluded that there aren't any, since 80 does not divide into 360 evenly. When we were looking at regular polygons last week, we saw that if you have, like, a pentagon, you can make five triangles, and each has a 72-degree angle. So if you turn the triangle 72 degrees, it will match. But you can't do that with 80. So it won't work.

Teacher: What did the rest of the groups conclude?

Example 16: Taking a Spin—*Continued*

Student 2:   That's what we thought at first. But then we thought about a 360-gon has a 1-degree angle and so it should be able to hit every degree, so if you rotate it 80 times, it will eventually work!

Student 1:   But is that possible? Eighty doesn't divide into 360, right?

The teacher asks the students to discuss this issue further in their small groups for a few minutes and then pulls the class back together, asking the groups to share their observations.

Student 3:   OK, we agree that 360 will work. Like they said, it will hit every degree. [He draws a rough sketch with many small sides.] If you rotate it once, it will match. But you can keep on going. [He mimics doing lots of very small rotations.] And when you do this 80 times, it will work.

Teacher: Is that really 80-degree rotational symmetry?

Student 3:   We rotated 80 degrees, and it matched up with itself.

Student 4:   We think that 2 degrees should work, too.

Teacher: What do you think they mean by that?

Student 4:   If you rotate it forty times, it will hit 80 degrees.

Student 5:   But you can't have a 2-gon! That wouldn't even be a polygon.

Student 4:   Oh.

Student 6:   It's not a 2-gon, it has a 2 degree angle. So if you divide 2 into 360, that would be a 180-gon.

The class continues to discuss the situation and finally agrees that both regular 360-gons and 180-gons will work. Students suggest other regular polygons that they think will work, and the teacher ends the discussion by assigning students the task of finding all regular polygons that have 80-degree rotational symmetry. He asks them to write up their findings in a short essay that they can share with their classmates the next day. The essay should both give all the regular polygons that they have found and prove that they have in fact found them all.

Key Elements of Mathematics

Reasoning with Geometry—Conjecturing about geometric objects; Construction and evaluation of geometric arguments; Multiple geometric approaches

Reasoning Habits

Analyzing a problem—identifying concepts, representations, or procedures; considering special cases or simpler analogs

Implementing a strategy—monitoring progress toward a solution

Reflection on a solution—reconciling different approaches; justifying or validating a solution; refining arguments

The idea of geometric transformations forges a link between geometry and other concepts of mathematics, such as the general concept of functions and the use of matrices in their representations.

Geometric Connections and Modeling

The use of coordinate geometry to justify geometric properties is an important merging of geometry and algebra. But, as mentioned in chapter 2, geometric ideas also connect with many ideas in other mathematical domains. Such connections arise naturally and profitably in mathematical modeling situations. Example 17 contains a sequence of tasks that involve students in the four parts of the modeling cycle diagrammed in figure 2.1 in chapter 2. In this example, ideas from geometry, trigonometry, algebra, functions, number, and measurement all play a role in a modeling problem that is quite simple to state and begin but that becomes increasingly complex. The example involves a problem encountered in everyday life: a truck getting stuck under a bridge. In tasks 1 and 2 students collect some information (about road grades, for instance) and create a mathematical model with simplifying assumptions (see parts 1 and 2 of the modeling cycle in fig. 2.1).

Example 17: Clearing the Bridge

Task 1

Mathematician Henry Pollak (2004) pondered why tractor trailers often got stuck under a certain underpass when the "maximum clearance" was clearly labeled by a sign that indicated the height of the bridge. The bridge under consideration was level and located just at the base of a descending road. In this initial task students are asked to construct a two-dimensional visual model of the situation, listing assumptions that they make.

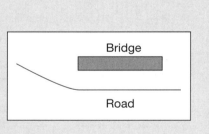

In the Classroom (Second-Year Mathematics)

In a visual model, one set of trailer wheels is jacked up on the sloping part of the road as the truck passes under the edge of the bridge. This position causes a portion of the trailer to be raised higher than it would be on a flat surface. The real question is, How much higher? The model that students construct likely will include

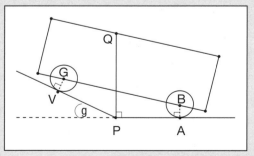

characteristics similar to the model in the diagram at the right. Such a model should at least contain the line segment *PQ*—representing the "dangerous height" at which the trailer might hit the bridge. The model pictured here contains simplifying assumptions, such as representation of the wheels as circles and representation of the road as two straight line

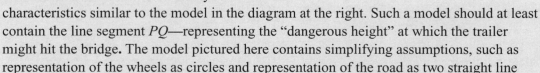

Example 17: Clearing the Bridge—*Continued*

segments. Each simplifying assumption deserves discussion in class. In addition, after a fruitful discussion, the class may decide to measure the road grade in terms of degrees rather than as a percent. This decision is enacted in the analysis that follows. Some research by students may suggest that for most roadways, the road grade can reasonably be limited to what appears to be a small measure. In the present model, the road grade, *g,* is limited to 7 degrees—at least in this iteration of the modeling cycle. (Although a grade angle of 7 degrees may be steep for a large truck, some diagrams here include a much larger grade angle to illuminate detail.)

After students work on the construction of a model, an interactive computer model can be given to students so that they can explore how changes in various trailer dimensions and positions can affect the dangerous height, *PQ.* One of these variables is the distance the trailer is under the bridge. Another, more subtle variable is the distance between the wheel axles. (By itself, the overhang of the trailer beyond either wheel axle does not affect the dangerous height and can be ignored.)

The next decision made by this class was to simplify the model even further during the first trip through the modeling cycle, taking the wheels off the truck. See the simplified model at the right. (The supporting topic book on geometry offers an analysis of the situation that uses the full model with the wheels on.)

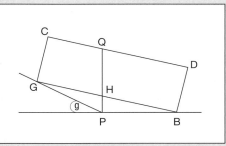

Task 2

Task 2 asks the students to examine what might be lost or misrepresented by this simplification. We do not provide a detailed classroom discussion of task 2. However, students should realize that taking the wheels off and lowering the shortened trailer box does not simply lower the dangerous height by an amount equal to the wheel radius. Rather, the left (raised) end of the truncated trailer box is lowered a bit more than the right end, and this positioning does have an additional measurable effect on the dangerous height. Nevertheless, an analysis of the simplified model will help us analyze the original situation with the more complex model, in which the trailer has wheels. Moreover, even in this simpler case with a small grade angle, the result may be surprising.

Tasks 3 and 4 ask students to explore relationships in the simplified model both geometrically and symbolically.

Task 3

Let *d* represent the length of segment *PQ, w* represent the measure of angle *PBH* (the tilt of the trailer), *s* represent the length of segment *PB* (how far the trailer is under the bridge),

Example 17: Clearing the Bridge—*Continued*

and *g* represent the grade in degrees. Explore the situation by using your interactive drawing of the simplified model. See if you can get a feel for—or make a conjecture about—when the dangerous height, *d,* would be highest by considering *w* or *s* or both.

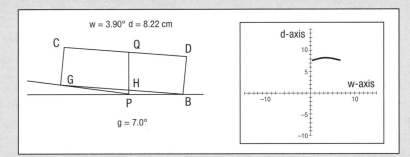

In the Classroom (Second-Year Mathematics)

One group used the interactive drawing to trace the graph of the dangerous height, *d,* as a function of *w,* as seen in the figure above, where they have set *g* equal to 7 degrees. They noted that they were not able to find a symbolic representation of this function but that it did suggest useful information. In their exploration, they used several small values of *g,* and each time the dangerous height looked greatest when

$$w = \frac{g}{2}.$$

Another group used large angles for grades, for instance, 55 degrees, and that pattern did not hold up. But other students raised the objection that such large grades were unrealistic and not within bounds of the model. More insight was sought about what happens for small values of *g.*

After additional work, group 3 presented some theoretical evidence that adds some insight and support to the claim that the maximum value of the dangerous height occurs when

$$w = \frac{g}{2}$$

for the (small) values of *g* that our model allows.

Group 3 drew an analogy to example 15, "Circling the Points," and envisioned $\angle GPB$ inscribed in a circle together with chord *GB*. The first thing to note is that the point *P* changes position along the arc of the circle as the trailer box is drawn along the roadway. The perpendicular distance from *P* to the chord *GB* is greatest when the foot of this perpendicular, *K,* is the midpoint of segment *GB*.

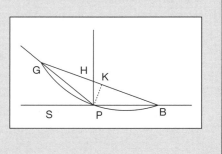

Example 17: Clearing the Bridge—*Continued*

Student 3: When K is the midpoint of segment GB, angles $\angle PGB$ and $\angle PBG$ are congruent. I know that $m\angle PGB + m\angle PBG = m\angle SPG$, and the measure of angle $\angle SPG = g$. So now I have that

$$m\angle PGB = m\angle PBG = \frac{g}{2} = w.$$

Now I want to show that the part of the dangerous height represented by segment PH is really close in length to segment PK—wherever K is on BG. That is because the angle between segment PK and segment PH is small if g is small. Here's why that is true. Triangles PHK and PHB are similar because they are right triangles that share $\angle PHK$. So $m\angle HPK = m\angle PBH = w$. But I know that $0 \le w \le g \le 7°$. Then $0.99 \le \cos(w) \le 1$. Since

$$\cos(w) - \cos(\angle PHK) = \frac{\left|PK\right|}{\left|PH\right|},$$

we've got that

$$0.99 \le \frac{\left|PK\right|}{\left|PH\right|} \le 1.$$

This means the two lengths in the fraction are really, really close. *The point is that part of the dangerous height represented by segment PH should be maximized when the length of segment PK is maximized, and that is when*

$$m\angle PBG = \frac{g}{2}.$$

Teacher: That gives some pretty solid support for the idea that there is at least a portion of the dangerous height that is at least close to being maximized when

$$w = \frac{g}{2}.$$

Let's continue by analyzing d a little further.

Task 4

Can you find a symbolic relationship between the tilt of the trailer, w, and the measure of the dangerous height d? You may use other measurements related to the model, such as s (the distance the trailer is under the bridge, measured by segment PB), the length of the shortened trailer box (measured by segment GB), or some other measurement related to the situation. You may continue to find trigonometry useful.

Example 17: Clearing the Bridge—*Continued*

In the Classroom (After Further Discussion)

Group 5:　　We did find trigonometry helpful. We found a relationship between the length of segment *PH* and *w* first. We got that

$$\tan(w) = \frac{|PH|}{|PB|}.$$

So $|PB| \tan(w) = |PH|$. That is, $s \cdot \tan(w) = |PH|$.

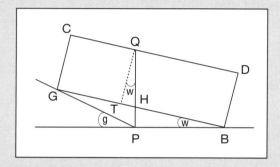

We wanted to find out something about the length of segment *HQ* next. We didn't get anywhere at first, but then one of our group members noticed that this segment sort of replaces the original height of the truck. So we decided to compare it to the original height of the truck. So then we drew segment *QT* perpendicular to *GB*. The length of segment *QT* would be the original height of the truck. After we drew the segment, we saw that ∠*PHB* and ∠*THQ* were congruent because they are vertical angles. That makes the right triangles *PHB* and *THQ* similar. So ∠*HQT* = *w*. We let *h* stand for the original height of the truck. That is, *h* = |*QT*|. So

$$\cos(w) = \frac{h}{|HQ|}.$$

This means that

$$|HQ| = \frac{h}{\cos(w)}.$$

Example 17: Clearing the Bridge—*Continued*

We put these together and got

$$d = s \cdot \tan(w) + \frac{h}{\cos(w)}.$$

Teacher: Good. That relationship works for any value of w that occurs within the model. Now it is time to think about interpreting these results in the real world. What value of g should we use in our formula?

Class: Seven degrees.

Teacher: We have gathered support for testing w at

$$\frac{g}{2},$$

or 3.5 degrees. For homework, research a good height to use for the trailer box and a good length for the trailer length between points G and B. In addition, for

$$w = \frac{g}{2}$$

and $|GB| = m,$ determine how one could figure out the value of s. We will need to do that to determine the value of d.

The next day students decide on $h = 10$ feet and $m = 40$ feet. In addition, $\triangle PGB$ is isosceles when

$$w = \frac{g}{2}.$$

By constructing the altitude from P to side $GB,$ one can derive the relationship

$$\cos(g/2) = \frac{m/2}{s} \quad \text{or} \quad s = \frac{m/2}{\cos(g/2)}.$$

With these values,

$$d = \frac{20}{\cos(3.5)} \tan(3.5) + \frac{10}{\cos(3.5)}$$

$$\approx 11.24 \text{ feet,}$$

or about 11 feet 3 inches. Just looking at the value 7 degrees as a small number might suggest that road grade does not matter. But our analysis for this specific and realistic example shows that with an initial trailer height of 10 feet, the dangerous height for the trailer is *at least a foot higher!* As Dr. Pollak noted, road grade cannot be ignored.

Example 17: Clearing the Bridge—*Continued*

Key Elements of Mathematics

Reasoning with Geometry—Geometric connections and modeling; Construction and
    evaluation of geometric arguments
Reasoning with Algebraic Symbols—Meaningful use of symbols; Mindful
    manipulation
Reasoning with Functions—Using multiple representations of functions

Reasoning Habits

Analyzing the problem—identifying relevant variables and conditions; seeking patterns and
    relationships; looking for hidden structure; considering special cases or simpler analogs
Implementing a strategy—making purposeful use of procedures; making logical
    deductions; monitoring progress toward a solution
Seeking and using connections
Reflecting on a solution—considering the reasonableness of a solution; justifying or
    validating a solution; reconciling different approaches; generalizing a solution

The geometry strand extends beyond two- and three-dimensional figures in Euclidean space to include other special configurations and visualizations. Example 18 illustrates a modeling context in which the most obvious geometric model of the situation—drawing circles of radius 5 units and looking for overlaps that represent radio interference—is not the most useful. Rather, a basic representation in the growing field of "graph theory"—usually considered a domain within discrete mathematics—is better suited to capture the relevant information in the modeling problem.

Example 18: Assigning Frequencies

Task

The Federal Communications Commission (FCC) needs to assign radio frequencies to seven new radio stations located on the grid at the right. Such assignments are based on several considerations, including the possibility of creating interference by assigning the same frequency to stations that are too close together. In this simplified situation, we assume that broadcasts from two stations located within 200 miles of each other will create interference if they broadcast on the

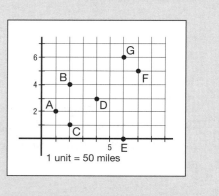

Example 18: Assigning Frequencies

same frequency, whereas stations more than 200 miles apart can use the same frequency to broadcast without causing interference with each other.

How can a vertex-edge graph be used to assign frequencies so that the fewest number of frequencies are used and no stations interfere with each other? What would each vertex represent? What would an edge represent? What is the fewest number of frequencies needed? (Adapted from Hirsch et al. [2007])

In the Classroom

Students work on the task in groups. Each group seems to agree that a vertex in the graph represents a radio station. So the graph would have seven vertices. Some groups decide to make a graph model in which two vertices representing stations within 200 miles of each other will be joined by an edge.

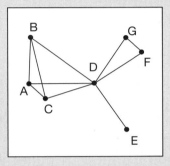

Other groups suggest that two vertices will be joined with an edge if they are *more* than 200 miles apart. After some discussion, the choice is made to use the first suggestion, that of joining vertices with an edge if the distance between them is no more than 200 miles. The next task is to construct the model. Doing so requires computation of the distance between each pair of stations. Groups make these computations by using the distance formula or Pythagorean theorem and a calculator. Organization is valuable here because many computations are involved. Some groups might start by computing the distance from *A* to the remaining six stations, then the distance from *B* to the remaining five, and so on. A quick determination of how many computations are needed can help determine whether any list is missing an item. Experience with example 10, "Patterns, Plane and Symbol," would be useful in this context.

Groups produce models similar to the one above and then work at assigning frequencies to vertices so that no two vertices joined by a single edge have the same frequency. They look for a method that will use the fewest frequencies for this particular graph. One group explained their solution this way:

"We found that the fewest number of frequencies that could be used was four. We reasoned this way: First, look at the collection of vertices *A* through *D*. Each of these vertices is joined by an edge to each of the other three in the collection. So no two vertices in the collection can have the same frequency. That means you can have no fewer than four frequencies.

"Next, suppose you assign frequency 1 to vertex *A,* frequency 2 to vertex *B,* frequency 3 to vertex *C,* and frequency 4 to vertex *D.* You can finish the assignment by assigning frequency 1 to vertex *G* (because *G* doesn't interfere with *A*), frequency 2 to vertex *F,* and frequency 3 to vertex *E.* That proves you don't need any more than four frequencies. That does it!"

Example 18: Assigning Frequencies —*Continued*

Key Elements of Mathematics

Reasoning with Geometry—Geometric connections and modeling; Construction of geometric arguments

Reasoning Habits

Analyzing a problem—seeking patterns and relationships; applying previously learned concepts

Implementing a strategy—organizing a solution; making logical deductions

Reflecting on a solution—justifying or validating a solution

Note that the vertex-edge representation of the frequency-assignment problem seems to have facilitated the structuring of an argument that four frequencies suffice—and even a way (algorithm) to assign four frequencies—for this example. Finding efficient algorithms for analogues of the general fewest-frequency problem for larger graphs remains an active area of current mathematical research. Such algorithms would find uses in many contexts.

Geometry offers an inviting context in which students can develop their reasoning and sense-making abilities. In addition, geometry provides tools and representations that are useful in a wide range of situations.

Chapter 8

Reasoning with Statistics and Probability

IN OUR increasingly data-intensive world, statistics is one of the most important areas of the mathematical sciences for helping students make sense of the information all around them, as well as for preparing them for further study in a variety of disciplines (e.g., the health sciences, the social sciences, and environmental science) for which statistics is a fundamental tool for advancing knowledge. Competence in the Standards found in *Principles and Standards* (NCTM 2000a) depends on a thorough and deep understanding of the foundations of statistics and probability, and of the connections between statistics and probability. Taken together, *Principles and Standards* and the American Statistical Association's report *Guidelines for Assessment and Instruction in Statistics Education* (*GAISE*) (Franklin et al. 2007) describe statistical problem solving as an investigative process that involves the following four components:

- Formulating a question (or questions) that can be addressed with data
- Designing and employing a plan for collecting data
- Analyzing and summarizing the data
- Interpreting the results from the analysis, and answering the question on the basis of the data

The common thread throughout the statistical problem-solving process is the focus on making sense of, and reasoning about, variation in data. The goal is not only to solve problems in the presence of variation but also to provide a measure of how much the variation might affect the solution. This process provides a framework for teaching and learning statistics in school, and meaningful tasks that employ this process should permeate the statistical education of our students.

Key elements of reasoning and sense making with statistics and probability include the following:

- *Data analysis.* Gaining insight about a solution to a statistics question by collecting data and describing features of the data through the use of graphical and tabular representations and numerical summaries. (The interpretation of results in data analysis encompasses both empirical and informal levels of reasoning, as described in the progression of reasoning in chapter 2.)
- *Modeling variability.* Developing probability models to describe the long-run behavior of observations of a random variable.

- *Connecting statistics and probability*. Recognizing probability as an essential tool of statistics; understanding the role of probability in statistical reasoning.
- *Interpreting designed statistical studies*. Drawing appropriate conclusions from data in ways that acknowledge random variation. (Interpreting results from designed statistical studies involves statistical inference and other more formal levels of statistical reasoning.)

We address these key elements in more detail in the following sections.

Data Analysis

Data analysis is more than simply the analysis of data. Data analysis includes all four components described in the process of statistical problem solving. Data are observations or measurements collected on one or more variables to address a statistical question. In statistics, a variable is any characteristic for which individual observations can be expected to take different values. Consequently, data vary and, once collected, need to be summarized in ways that foster meaningful insights for addressing the question under study. The analysis of data includes exploring various representations of the *data distribution* to summarize and describe patterns and relationships in the variation and to identify deviations from a pattern. Technology provides the opportunity to examine various representations of the data distribution and to identify important features of the distribution. In data analysis, the interpretation of results includes both empirical and informal levels of reasoning. Because both numerical data and numerical summaries of data are used in data analysis, statistics has connections with the Numbers and Measurements strand described in chapter 4, particularly the key elements of *reasonableness of answers and measurements* and *approximations and error*.

Example 19 shows how statistical procedures for analyzing data that are developed in earlier grades continue to be useful tools for making sense of, and reasoning about, data in high school. Example 19 illustrates organizing and interpreting a solution and recognizing the scope of inference for a statistical solution. A detailed description of this activity is given in Kader and Mamer (2008).

Example 19: Meaningful Words, Part A
Adapted from WGBH Educational Foundation (2001)

Task

Scientists are interested in human recall and memory. Is it easier to memorize words that have "meaning?" To study this problem, two lists of 20 three-letter "words" were used. One list contained meaningful words (e.g., CAT, DOG), whereas the other list contained nonsense words (e.g., ATC, ODG). A ninth-grade class of thirty students was randomly divided into two groups of fifteen students. One group was asked to memorize the list of meaningful words; the other group was asked to memorize the list of nonsense words. The number of words correctly recalled by each student was tabulated, and the resulting data are as follows:

Example 19: Meaningful Words, Part A—*Continued*

Number of meaningful words recalled: 12, 15, 12, 12, 10, 3, 7, 11, 9, 14, 9, 10, 9, 5, 13
Number of nonsense words recalled: 4, 6, 6, 5, 7, 5, 4, 7, 9, 10, 4, 8, 7, 3, 2

1. Provide a display for summarizing and comparing these data sets.

2. On the basis of your display, what observations can be made regarding how the students assigned the meaningful words performed compared with how the students assigned the nonsense words performed? Write a paragraph summarizing what the data and your analysis reveal about the question "Is it easier to memorize words that have meaning?"

In the Classroom (Ninth-Grade Mathematics Class)

Several groups of students created comparative dotplots for the data, as shown below.

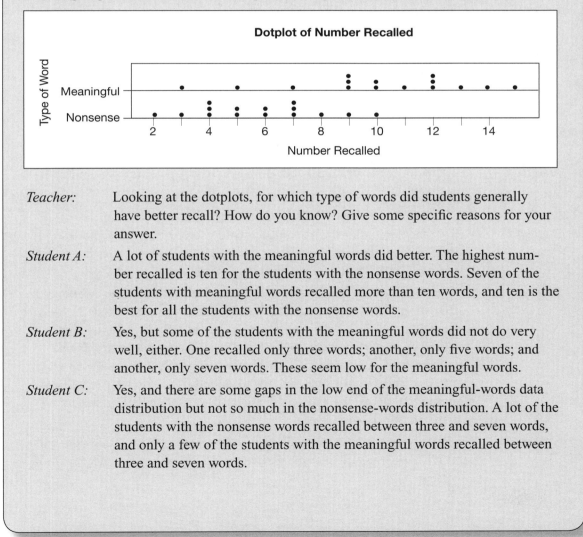

Teacher: Looking at the dotplots, for which type of words did students generally have better recall? How do you know? Give some specific reasons for your answer.

Student A: A lot of students with the meaningful words did better. The highest number recalled is ten for the students with the nonsense words. Seven of the students with meaningful words recalled more than ten words, and ten is the best for all the students with the nonsense words.

Student B: Yes, but some of the students with the meaningful words did not do very well, either. One recalled only three words; another, only five words; and another, only seven words. These seem low for the meaningful words.

Student C: Yes, and there are some gaps in the low end of the meaningful-words data distribution but not so much in the nonsense-words distribution. A lot of the students with the nonsense words recalled between three and seven words, and only a few of the students with the meaningful words recalled between three and seven words.

Example 19: Meaningful Words, Part A—*Continued*

Teacher: Can you be more specific?

Student C: Well, three out of the fifteen students with the meaningful words recalled between three and seven words. That's only 20 percent. For the students using the nonsense words, eleven out of fifteen, more than 73 percent, recalled that many. If you add the student who only recalled two nonsense words, twelve out of these fifteen students, that's 80 percent, recalled between two and seven words, whereas only 20 percent of the students with the meaningful words were this low. In fact, all fifteen students using the nonsense words recalled between two and ten words, but only eight students with the meaningful words were this low.

Teacher: That's the same as what student A said, seven of the fifteen students using the meaningful-words list recalled more words than any of the students using the nonsense-words list. That means close to half the students memorizing the meaningful words did better than all students with the nonsense words.

Teacher: Let's try to identify a typical value for the number of words recalled for each list. What quantity would you propose?

Student D: We could find the average number recalled for each list.

Teacher: Why do you propose the average, which is also called the *mean*?

Student D: Well, it seems like we always find the mean whenever we want to know a typical value.

Student E: Yes, sometimes the mean is good. But sometimes we use the median for a typical value.

Teacher: In this case, does it matter which one you use?

Student E: Well, in the dotplot for the meaningful words, three of the values look kind of small. I think these three values might make the mean smaller than what's typical. So I would use the median instead of the mean.

Teacher: Very good. When we see a graph of data like the dotplot for the meaningful words, we say the shape of the data distribution is skewed to the left. Like student E said, when a data distribution is skewed left, the mean is often smaller than what one might think of as typical for the data. For this reason, the median might provide a better indication of how many words were typically recalled by students with the meaningful list. So, what would you propose for a typical value for the number of words recalled by students with the nonsense-words list?

Student E: The data distribution for the nonsense list looks pretty even. I think this indicates it has a symmetrical shape. So you could probably use either the mean

Example 19: Meaningful Words, Part A—*Continued*

or the median for these data. Since we are using the median for the meaningful words, and it would not make sense to compare the mean of one group to the median of another group, I would use the median for the nonsense words as well.

Teacher: What do the rest of you think? What happens when we use the medians?

Student D: My calculator gives the median for the meaningful words as 10, and for the nonsense words the median is 6.

Teacher: What if we did not have the data values, but only knew the medians? What do the medians tell us about the data?

Student D: The median divides the data in half.

Teacher: Yes, so if the median is ten words for the data on meaningful words, what can we say about the rest of the data?

Student F: About half the students assigned to the meaningful-words list remembered fewer than ten words, and about half remembered more than ten words.

Teacher: Comparing the two medians, what would you conclude?

Student F: The median for the meaningful words is ten words, but the median for the nonsense words is six words. Ten is higher than six, so students with meaningful words typically did better than the students with nonsense words.

Teacher: This is an interesting observation. Another way of looking at this is to say that the difference between the medians is four words. So students with the meaningful words typically recalled four more words than students with the nonsense list.

Teacher: If only the medians are reported for these data, what information about the number of words recalled is missing?

Student G: If all you know is the median, you don't know the actual number recalled for each student. Take the data for the meaningful words. If all I know is that the median number recalled is ten words, I don't really know about the different values that actually occurred. For example, looking at the student who remembered only three words, three words is a lot different from ten words.

Teacher: So, student G, what is the idea you talking about called?

Student G: The number of words recalled is not the same for each student. I think this is the idea of variability in the data, which we have talked about before.

Teacher: Yes, you are correct. In statistics, we are interested in representing the data with a typical value, such as the median, but we are also interested in summarizing the amount of variability in the data, as well. Does anyone have any suggestions for how we might do this?

Example 19: Meaningful Words, Part A—*Continued*

Student H: We could find the ranges. I think this tells us something about how much variability there is. The range is 12 for the meaningful list. The range for the nonsense list is 8.

Teacher: So, what do the ranges suggest about the variation in the data?

Student H: The biggest difference between any two values from the meaningful list is twelve words, but the biggest difference between any two values from the nonsense list is eight words. This says that there is more variability in the number of words recalled on the meaningful words list than on the nonsense words list.

Student I: Yes, but the smallest value from the meaningful words seems really small. For this reason, I don't think I would use the ranges. Instead, I think we should find the quartiles and use the interquartile ranges (IQR) instead. Then I am comparing the amount of variation for the middle portions of each group.

Teacher: How do you find the IQR?

Student I: First you have to find the first and third quartiles for each group of data. Then you find the range between the quartiles. You subtract the first quartile from the third quartile.

Teacher: OK. Everyone find the quartiles and the interquartile ranges.

Student J: For the meaningful words, my calculator gives the first quartile as nine words and the third quartile as twelve words. So the IQR is three words. For the nonsense words, the first quartile is four words and the third quartile is seven words. So the IQR is three words. The IQRs are the same, so there are similar amounts of variation in the middle 50 percent of the data for both the meaningful words and the nonsense words.

Student K: My calculator gives five quantities for each group—the minimum, the first quartile, the median, the third quartile, and the maximum. I think we can get a graph called a *box-and-whiskers plot* by using these five numbers.

Teacher: Yes, you can. When you include an outlier analysis, it is called a *modified boxplot*.

The class used results from a calculator to produce the following comparative modified boxplots:

Example 19: Meaningful Words, Part A—*Continued*

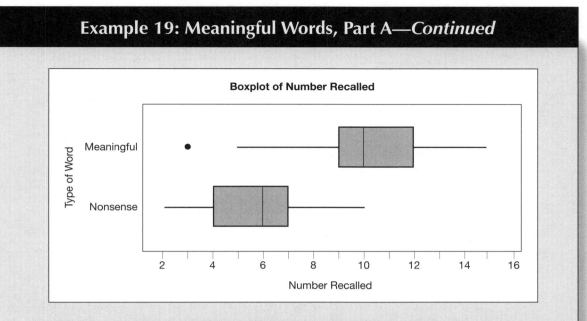

Teacher: Can you use the results from the boxplots to summarize our discussions about this question?

Student M: Students with the list of meaningful words generally recalled more words. The maximum number of words recalled for the students with the nonsense list is ten. Ten is the median number recalled for the meaningful list, so about half the students with the meaningful words recalled more words than any of the student with the nonsense words. With the meaningful words, one student recalled only three words, and this score is an outlier and somewhat lower than expected when compared to the other data. The median number recalled with the meaningful words is ten, which is four more words than the median number recalled from the nonsense words. Excluding the outlier from the meaningful-words data, both groups appear to have similar amounts of variation. The IQR for each group is 3, indicating that for both meaningful and nonsense words the number of words recalled within the middle 50 percent differ by no more than three words.

Teacher: What do these results suggest about memory and meaning?

Student N: Since students with the meaningful words seemed to do better, these data suggest it is easier to memorize words that have meaning.

Teacher: Do you think it would be appropriate to say that all ninth graders would get exactly the same results?

Student O: Sure, it's easier to memorize words that have meaning.

Student P: Well, we would not get *exactly* the same scores! But we might still see that words with meaning will be easier to memorize.

Example 19: Meaningful Words, Part A—*Continued*

Teacher: We have to be careful about our scope of inference, or trying to generalize these results to other ninth graders based on these data. The scope of inference depends on whether or not the studied class is representative of all ninth-grade classes. As we don't know how the class was selected, we should not try to generalize the results to all ninth-grade classes or to all ninth graders. If a group of ninth-grade students is selected at random, then we might try to generalize these results to all ninth graders.

Student Q: But I thought they used randomness in the study.

Teacher: Yes, they did. However, randomness was used in assigning the students to the different groups. The reason for using random assignment is to produce two comparable groups. For example, you would not want all students who are good at memorizing in one group. By randomly assigning the students to the two groups, we hope to balance the effects from not only students' memorizing ability but from any other variables that might be related to the number of words recalled. Although random assignment does not guarantee similar groups, there is a high likelihood of creating groups that are similar groups with regard to all variables.

Key Elements of Mathematics

Reasoning with Statistics and Probability—Data analysis

Reasoning Habits

Analyzing a Problem—deciding whether a statistical approach is appropriate; identifying relevant concepts, procedures, or representations; seeking patterns and relationships; making preliminary deductions and conjectures

Implementing a strategy—organizing the solution

Seeking and using connections

Reflecting on a solution—interpreting a solution; justifying or validating a solution; recognizing the scope of inference

Modeling Variability

Probability models reinforce the foundational principle that although an individual observation of a random variable cannot be predicted with certainty, patterns emerge in the frequency of values over a large number of observations. Fostering students' understanding of random variables and probability requires engaging them in the development of both simulation and mathematical probability models. The design of a simulation model requires that students set up a logical sequence of steps for describing the possible outcomes of a random variable. The implementation of a simulation model allows students to both experience and make sense of the notion of the long-run behavior of a random variable and to determine experimental probabilities. The design and implementation of a simulation also provides transitional steps in the development of reasonable mathematical models for describing the long-run behavior of a random variable. Because many probability models involve counting, probability has connections with the Numbers and Measurements strand and the key element of *counting* described in chapter 4. Example 20 considers various developmental strategies for arriving at a solution to a probability problem and illustrates the importance of identifying relevant concepts, procedures, or representations and knowing how a solution can be generalized to a broader class of problems.

Example 20: What Are the Chances? Part A

Task

A high school club has fifty members: ten girls and forty boys. The refreshments committee will be formed by selecting two students from the club at random. What is the probability of getting exactly zero girls on the committee? Exactly one girl on the committee? Exactly two girls on the committee? That is, if two students are repeatedly selected at random from the club, how often will exactly no girl be selected? Exactly one girl? Exactly two girls?

In the Classroom (Ninth- to Twelfth-Grade Mathematics Classes)

The class is instructed to design a hands-on simulation for estimating the probability for each of the different possible results for the number of girls on the committee. Prior to this activity, students should have had experiences performing simulations by using various random devices and random-number generators in graphing calculators. After the task is read, the teacher can ask the students how they might design a simulation for the situation of choosing two students for the committee and reporting the number of girls on the committee.

The teacher can lead a discussion to help students design the simulation. Students may propose the use of a standard deck of cards (they would remove two face cards and represent the girls with the ten remaining face cards and the boys with the forty non–face cards). For each trial, they would shuffle the deck several times and then select two cards. The number of face cards selected represents the number of girls on the committee. For the next trial, they would replace the cards in the deck, reshuffle, and select two more cards. Students would need to decide how many trials to perform. From previous experiences, students know that the relative frequencies tend to be close to the actual probabilities if they perform a large number of trials. Together, the class performed a simulation of two hundred trials. The results are summarized in the table at the top of the next page.

Example 20: What Are the Chances? Part A—*Continued*

Number of Girls	Frequency	Experimental Probability
0	121	.605
1	70	.350
2	9	.045
	200	1.000

The experimental probabilities provide estimates for the true probabilities for each of the different possible results and illustrate the long-run relative frequency interpretation of probability.

In the Classroom (High School Statistics Class)

Students can revisit this problem in a statistics class after they have learned about tree diagrams and are learning about rules of probability. The class constructed the tree diagram at the right for describing the gender of the two students selected.

Students are asked to describe the ordered sequence of outcomes for gender that results in the number of girls selected to be 0. For this outcome, the ordered sequence must be—

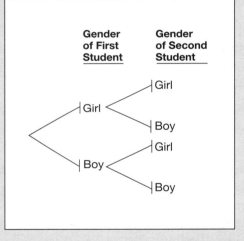

Boy selected first and boy selected second.

Students are asked to determine the probability that the first student selected is a boy, which they all agree is

$$\frac{40}{50},$$

or 0.8.

They are then asked to think about the probability that the second student selected is a boy, and many said

Example 20: What Are the Chances? Part A—*Continued*

$$\frac{39}{49}.$$

The teacher asks about any assumptions made in determining this probability, and the class agrees that this probability assumes that the first student selected is a boy. The teacher points out that

$$\frac{39}{49}$$

is called a "conditional" probability and represents the probability that the second student selected is a boy, given that the first student selected is a boy. The teacher then asks about the probability of the ordered sequence "Boy selected first and boy selected second." A student responds that the sequence can occur only if a boy is selected first and, given that a boy was selected first, a boy is selected second. That is,

$$
\begin{aligned}
P(0 \text{ Girls}) &= P(\text{Boy selected first and Boy selected second}) \\
&= P(\text{Boy selected first})P(\text{Boy selected second given Boy selected first}) \\
&= \frac{40}{50} \cdot \frac{39}{49}.
\end{aligned}
$$

The teacher uses this opportunity to present the product rule for probability:

$$P(A \text{ and } B) = P(A)P(B \text{ given that } A \text{ has occurred}).$$

The class expands the tree diagram to show the conditional probabilities for the outcome of gender at each stage of the selection, the ordered sequence of gender, and the number of girls selected for each ordered sequence.

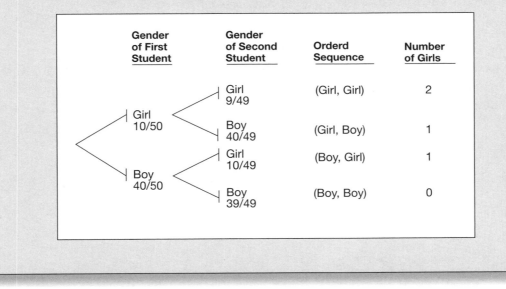

Example 20: What Are the Chances? Part A—*Continued*

By traversing the tree and using the product rule, the class determines each of the following probabilities:

P(No Girls) $= (40/50)(39/49) \approx .637,$
P(One Girl) $= (10/50)(40/49) + (40/50)(10/49) \approx .327,$ and
P(Two Girls) $= P$(Girl on First and Girl on Second) $= (10/50)(9/49) \approx .037.$

The teacher then asks the class to think about the following question for homework.

Suppose the gender of the first student selected is not known. We are interested in knowing the probability that the second student selected is a girl (regardless of the gender of the first student selected). This probability is—

$$P(\text{Girl selected Second}) = \frac{10}{50}.$$

Can you explain why this is the probability?

In the Classroom (Twelfth Grade)

Students can revisit this problem in the twelfth grade after they have learned counting rules. The class is instructed to use counting rules for determining the probability for each of the different possible results for the number of girls on the committee and to interpret the probabilities. Revisiting the same problem at a higher level gives students an opportunity to make sense of their earlier simulation.

Students are reminded that

$$C(m, k) = \frac{m!}{k!(m - k)!}$$

counts the number of subsets of size k from m distinct objects.

For this problem, we get $C(50, 2)$, or 1225, possible subsets (committees) of size two from the club of fifty students. Since the selection is random, we can assume that each possible committee is equally likely. The number of committees with—

exactly 0 girls (and exactly 2 boys) is $C(10, 0) \cdot C(40, 2)$, or 780;
exactly 1 girl (and exactly 1 boy) is $C(10, 1) \cdot C(40, 1)$, or 400;
exactly 2 girls (and exactly 0 boys) is $C(10, 2) \cdot C(40, 0)$, or 45.

Thus, the mathematical probabilities are as shown in the following table:

Example 20: What Are the Chances? Part A—*Continued*

Number of Girls	Probability
0	$\dfrac{780}{1225} \approx .637$
1	$\dfrac{400}{1225} \approx .327$
2	$\dfrac{45}{1225} \approx .037$

This example can be used as a rationale for developing the general formula for calculating these types of probabilities when sampling from a finite population. Suppose you have a population with N objects and each object is classified as either a success or a failure. Within the population, M of the objects are successes. You plan to randomly select n objects and to count the number of successes among those selected. For this situation, the number of successes is called a *hypergeometric random variable,* and the probability of obtaining exactly x successes is given by

$$P(x) = \frac{C(M,\, x) \cdot C(N-M,\, n-x)}{C(N,\, n)}.$$

Summary of example 20

Note that the estimated probabilities from the simulation in the first task are close to the probabilities obtained either through counting or using the tree diagram. These latter probabilities indicate that if two members are repeatedly selected at random from the club, then on any one trial, getting exactly zero girls is most likely and would occur approximately 64 percent of the time. Getting exactly one girl on the committee is fairly common and would occur approximately 33 percent of the time. In addition, since the probability of getting exactly two girls is less than .04, it would be unusual for the committee to have two girls.

An examination of this problem from a statistical perspective is described in example 21.

Key Elements of Mathematics

Reasoning with Statistics and Probability—Modeling variability
Number and Measurement—Counting

Reasoning Habits

Analyzing a problem—identifying relevant concepts, procedures, or representations
Implementing a strategy—making logical deductions
Seeking and using connections
Reflecting on one's solution—interpreting a solution; generalizing a solution

Connecting Statistics and Probability

By incorporating randomness into data collection, probability provides a way to make sense of the variation in sample results from one sample to another. The sampling distribution of a sample statistic (e.g., the sample mean, the sample median, the number of successes or the proportion of successes in the sample) summarizes the long-run behavior of the statistic from repeated random sampling. The sampling distribution provides a mechanism for describing the variation expected in a sample statistic and for determining whether an observed value might be reasonable from chance variation or whether it is more likely due to some other factor. The activity "Sampling Rectangles" in *Navigating through Data Analysis in Grades 9–12* (Burrill et al. 2003) illustrates important ideas related to the sampling distribution of the sample mean. The probability distribution developed in example 20 represents the sampling distribution for the number of girls (successes) in a random sample of size two selected from a club of fifty students with ten girls and forty boys. Sampling distributions make crucial links among data analysis, probability, and inferential reasoning in statistics. The following example illustrates foundational ideas underlying the reasoning in inferential statistics by considering the reasonableness of a solution and revisiting initial assumptions.

Example 21: What Are the Chances? Part B

In example 20 we looked at the hypothetical question of selecting two people for a committee and asking what might happen in terms of the number of girls selected. Suppose the president of the club forms the committee and both members are girls. We have now selected a sample and have data on the gender of each student selected. Reporting that the number of girls on the committee is two summarizes the sample data. After hearing the results, the girls in the club questioned the fairness in the selection of the committee. They pointed out that if the committee members were truly chosen at random, then the probability that both are girls is only .037 and, because this probability is small, a committee resulting in two girls is unlikely to occur. For this reason, they questioned whether the selection process was fair.

In the Classroom (Twelfth-Grade Mathematics Class)

This type of reasoning is the foundation for statistical inference. In this example we assume that the committee-selection process is truly random, and we use this assumption to determine the probability (sampling) distribution for the number of girls on the committee. We then ask how likely the observed result (two girls) is on the basis of this probability distribution. Because this probability is small, the data cast doubt on the assumption that the selection is truly random and thus fair.

Key Elements of Mathematics

Reasoning with Statistics and Probability—Connecting statistics and probability

Reasoning Habits

Seeking and using connections
Reflecting on a solution—considering the reasonableness of a solution; revisiting initial assumptions

Interpreting Designed Statistical Studies

Statistical inference involves drawing conclusions from, and making decisions based on, data obtained through designed sample surveys or experiments. Students should understand that the scope of inference for a study is related to the manner in which the data are collected. Data from studies that properly use random selection (sample surveys) or random assignment (experiments) can be used to estimate population characteristics from sample results or to determine whether a result is statistically significant. Sampling distributions offer a way to quantify the uncertainty associated with statistical inference. The reasoning employed in statistical inference is often quite difficult for students; however, using a simulation to create a sampling distribution offers an intuitive way to help students develop inferential reasoning skills. The following example illustrates the reasoning employed in designing and interpreting a simulation for detecting whether a statistically significant difference exists between two groups and presents an interpretation of a solution under uncertain conditions.

Example 22: Meaningful Words, Part B

Task
In example 19, the difference between the medians for the number of words recalled (Meaningful – Nonsense) was four words, and the fact that this difference is positive lends support to the conjecture that students tend to do better recalling meaningful words than they do recalling nonsense words. Random assignment was used to divide the class into two groups in the hope of producing comparable groups. That is, random assignment is likely to produce two similar groups with regard to all variables at the beginning of the study, and the only difference between the two groups at the end of the study is that one received meaningful words to memorize and the other received nonsense words. Probability provides a way to assess the strength of the evidence found in the difference between the medians. Specifically, because random assignment should produce similar groups, is the observed difference between the medians reasonable from the chance variation that occurs from random assignment, or is this difference likely to be due to the fact that one list contained meaningful words and the other list contained nonsense words?

Design and implement a simulation to address this question.

In the Classroom (Twelfth-Grade Class)
Students are assumed to have had some exposure to random assignment as a method for controlling for confounding variables and for creating comparable groups in an experimental study. After a class discussion, students reasoned that if the different lists (meaningful and nonsense words) have no effect on memorization, then the observed difference between the medians is due only to the variability expected from the random assignment to groups (i.e., due to the fact that student-to-student differences will be present). Note that a similar type of reasoning was employed in example 21 when students assumed that the selection process was truly random.

Example 22: Meaningful Words, Part B—*Continued*

If the different lists have no effect on memorization, then a student's score does not depend on whether he or she memorized meaningful words or nonsense words. Consequently, the number of words recalled by a student would be the same regardless of the group assigned. This situation can be simulated by writing each of the thirty scores on index cards (one score per card), shuffling the cards, and dealing out fifteen cards. The fifteen cards dealt represent scores for the meaningful words; the remaining fifteen cards represent the scores for the nonsense words. The median for each group and the difference between the two medians (meaningful – nonsense) can be determined. Because the original conjecture for this problem is that people will perform better with meaningful words, we are interested in knowing how often this difference is +4 or more. Repeating this simulation 100 times produced the simulated sampling distribution shown in the dotplot below for the difference between the two medians.

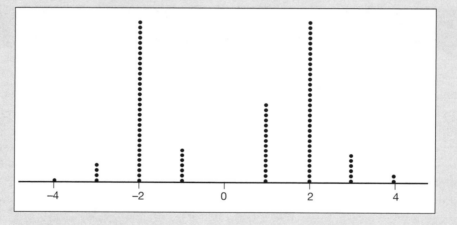

On the basis of this simulation, when no difference is assumed between the effects of the two types of words on memorization, a difference between medians of +4 or more occurred only two times out of 100 trials. This result suggests that a difference between medians this large (+4) or larger is unlikely to occur from chance variation alone. Thus, this difference between medians would be unusual when no difference exists between the effects of the two types of words on memorization; so the use of meaningful words does seem to help when trying to memorize.

Because this argument is based on a simulation of only 100 trials, the statistical reasoning employed here is transitional in nature, from informal to formal. If similar results occurred after performing the simulation with a *large number of trials,* or if the exact probability distribution for the difference between the medians was available and indicated a similar small probability for a difference of +4 or more, then we could say that the difference between the medians is *statistically significant* (would not be expected as a result of chance

Example 22: Meaningful Words, Part B—*Continued*

variation). In this example the data provide fairly strong evidence that the use of meaningful words does help when trying to memorize.

(A more detailed illustration of students' reasoning in this problem is presented in the supporting topic book on statistics and probability.)

Key Elements of Mathematics

Reasoning with Statistics and Probability—Modeling variability; Connecting statistics and probability; Interpreting designed statistical studies

Reasoning Habits

Analyzing a problem—deciding whether a statistical solution is appropriate; making preliminary deductions and conjectures; seeking patterns and relationships

Implementing a strategy—making purposeful use of procedures; organizing the solution; making logical deductions

Seeking and using connections

Reflecting on a solution—revisiting initial assumptions; justifying or validating a solution; interpreting a solution

Reasoning and Sense Making in the High School Mathematics Program

Equity

*Mathematical reasoning and sense making must
be evident in the mathematical experiences
of all students.*

IN THIS publication, we build on the concept of equity as defined in *Principles and Standards for School Mathematics* (NCTM 2000a), in which equity is described in terms of having high expectations of, and providing support for, all students. This population includes students of all races and cultures; students with low socioeconomic backgrounds; students whose first language is not English; both girls and boys; both gifted and low-achieving students; and students with learning disabilities, emotional problems, and behavioral problems. All too frequently, one or another of these groups is deemed too difficult to teach. Often, well-meaning teachers and administrators cause inequity through practices that create biases they do not intend. High schools can monitor equity by paying focused attention to phenomena that pose potential barriers to engaging every student in reasoning and sense making. These phenomena include the following:

- The *courses* that students take have an impact on the opportunities that they have for reasoning and sense making.

- *Students' demographics* too often predict the opportunities students have for reasoning and sense making

- *Expectations, beliefs, and biases* have an impact on the mathematical learning opportunities provided for students.

Courses

Over the past two decades, enrollment in advanced and college-preparatory mathematics courses at the high school level has increased noticeably (Planty, Provasnik, and Daniel 2007). At the same time, high schools have continued to employ some form of tracking or ability grouping (Hallinan 2004). With the tracking of students, high schools run the risk of promoting inequitable opportunities for mathematical learning for those students placed in remedial classes or in classes on "low" or "regular" tracks. For example, teacher quality varies across tracks, with more out-of-field teachers assigned to teach low-track classes (Tate and Rousseau 2002). High schools that use tracking or ability grouping can be proactive by diligently ensuring that at every level, all mathematics courses offer students opportunities for reasoning and sense making. In addition, with proper school support and access to such opportunities, students do not have to be mired in one track for their entire high school career. Successful high schools make sure that moves to different tracks are both offered and actively supported (Education Trust 2005). Moreover, we find numerous success stories of schools that have eliminated tracking with very positive results, including gains in mathematics course taking and achievement (Garrity 2004) and large numbers of minority students going on to attend college (Alvarez and Mehan 2006). An important point to note is that these schools' success was not attributed solely to eliminating tracking but to other elements of support for students and teachers in the schools, as well.

Schools with a curricular structure in which multiple levels of the same class are offered (e.g., Informal Geometry vs. Honors Geometry or Honors Integrated Mathematics vs. Integrated Mathematics) have a responsibility to engage all students in every class in reasoning and sense making, thereby ensuring that the students are learning the same major concepts regardless of the course title.

Students' unpreparedness for algebra is a current problem for high schools and often leads to schools' needing to provide some sort of remediation or additional academic support. Schools deal with this problem in various ways, such as stretching algebra over two years or placing students in a prealgebra class. These strategies can be counterproductive, especially if the result is that students are confined to the low track with limited attention to reasoning for the duration of high school and without the opportunity to catch up to their peers. High schools can support students who are underprepared for first-year algebra without limiting their future progress. For example, some high schools take early action with struggling students by offering courses in the summer before high school or as part of after-school programs (Education Trust 2005). Other schools provide first-year algebra students with general academic support in the form of teacher and peer tutoring, Saturday programs, and double course periods for some courses (Huebner, Corbett, and Phillippo 2006). In all instances, these high schools provide support early on for those students entering high school below grade level. Although programs to support underprepared students require additional resources, schools must make additional instruction to assist these students a priority. Algebra presents great opportunities for sense making and reasoning and lays a foundation for further study in mathematics. Thus, taking steps to ensure that all first-year algebra students are supported in ways that allow them to become proficient with algebraic concepts is of crucial importance.

The increasing emphasis on assessment in schools under the No Child Left Behind (NCLB) Act of 2001 (Public Law 107-110) has important consequences for opportunities for students to engage in reasoning and sense making in the classroom. In most instances, district and school policies on assessment heavily influence decisions about curriculum in the classroom. With extreme pressure for students to perform well on state assessments, teachers find themselves spending more time teaching test-taking skills and reviewing or covering those topics that are likely to be on the test. This emphasis, coupled with the fact that often high-stakes tests focus on students' ability to do procedural tasks rather assess their reasoning and sense making, equates to students' spending less time in class on developing their reasoning and sense-making abilities. This effect is even more prevalent for teachers in low-performing, high-minority schools who, under NCLB, often have even more pressure to ensure that their students succeed (Tate and Rousseau 2006). Coherence among assessment, curricula, and instruction is instrumental to addressing this issue. A discussion about the importance of coherence is included in chapter 11.

To ensure that this publication's vision becomes a reality, teachers must hold high expectations for all students and find strategies to ensure that all students, at any level and in any course, can reason mathematically by engaging in challenging mathematical tasks. One such strategy is using problems that have multiple entry points so that students at different levels of mathematical experience and with different interests can all engage meaningfully in reasoning about the problem. Using problems with multiple entry points allows students to use their individual mathematical strengths in approaching the problem and gives them opportunities to make sense of the reasoning of other students.

Several examples in section 2 of this publication describe tasks that have multiple entry points. For instance, example 7, "Finding Balance," presents a problem that can be solved with or without the use of equations. If students are able to use equations flexibly, as student 1 can in the example, they can represent the described situation symbolically, solve the equation, and find the solution. However, other students who are either less confident, have had limited experience with equations, or are unable to use them flexibly might approach the problem by first drawing a picture to represent the scenario, then move toward writing an equation. Others might use a more informal reasoning approach, such as the one used by student 2, to find the answer. Exploring multiple approaches to solving a problem can forge important connections among different mathematical domains and strengthen the reasoning abilities of all learners. In example 7, student 1's solution may help student 2 consider a more formal approach, and student 2's solution may help student 1 make sense of formal equation solving. For this reason, students should be given opportunities to discuss their different approaches with one another and work toward understanding how each approach relates to the others.

In any given high school classroom, students manifest varied levels of readiness for mathematical content, both among those who need extra support and among those who are ready to go further than the rest of the class. Often, students are deemed "gifted" or mathematically "talented" on the basis of a series of tests. However, teachers and schools should realize that students' mathematical "talent" is fluid (Samuels 2008) and that although a student might show great promise in geometry, for example, she or he might need extra support with algebraic content. For those students who demonstrate readiness to move beyond the core curriculum, teachers can provide opportunities to delve more deeply into the content being studied by the rest of the class. These students must have opportunities for reasoning and sense making that maximize their mathematical learning experiences. Although acceleration is definitely one component, opportunities for enrichment, advanced content, and more in-depth study can all be part of the mathematical education of these students, as well (National Association for Gifted Children 1994). For instance, in example 15, "Circling the Points," students discuss the result that three noncollinear points in a plane determine a unique circle. As a next step for a student who is interested or is ready to move beyond the task posed to the rest of the class, the teacher might pose the questions "Do four noncollinear points in the plane determine a unique circle?" "What are the conditions?" "What are some conjectures?" This series of questions leads the student to thinking about inscribed angles, a topic that would typically not be discussed in the course until later. Thus, the student is asked to think more deeply about the original problem assigned to the class.

Student Demographics and Opportunities for Learning

Discrepancies in achievement between student groups continue to raise concern for educators, families, and leaders in the United States. As reported on the mathematics portion of the 2003 National Assessment of Educational Progress (NAEP) (Lubienski and Crockett 2007), 52 percent of Hispanic and 61 percent of African American eighth-grade students scored below the basic level as compared with 20 percent of white eighth-grade students. Only 7 percent of African American students and 12 percent of Hispanic students scored at or above the proficient level in comparison with 37 percent of white students. An important finding of the same study was that white (91 percent) students were more likely to have fully credentialed teachers than African American (80 percent) and Hispanic (83 percent) students. This finding, coupled with the fact that students of teachers who majored in mathematics in college scored seven to fifteen points higher on NAEP than students of teachers who were not mathematics majors (Lubienski and Crockett 2007), indicates an important connection between discrepancies in resources and achievement.

Educators in the United States continue to grapple with economic inequity, which has a significant impact on districts' and schools' abilities to improve the opportunities to learn for the country's most underserved students (Tate and Rousseau 2007). Astounding discrepancies remain between the amount of money spent by the wealthiest districts as compared with that spent by the poorest, often high-minority, urban districts (Darling-Hammond 2004). These discrepancies exist between states as well as within states. Districts that spend more money often have smaller class sizes and more instructional resources, are able to offer a wider range of classes, and have teachers who are better paid and more experienced (Darling-Hammond 2004).

Providing students with more opportunities to learn mathematics has serious financial consequences. For example, creating Saturday or summer programs to provide additional support to those students not ready for algebra requires additional money. Unfortunately, such programs are needed most in schools or districts that often have fewer resources. Similarly, schools that are predominantly low-income, African American, or Hispanic often contend with high teacher-turnover rates. High turnover has the unfortunate consequence that those students who are most in need of the best possible teachers are very often being taught by the least experienced teachers (Bishop and Forgasz 2006). In addition, teaching out of field is more prevalent in high-minority and low-socioeconomic schools than in other schools, with the result that poor, minority students in the United States are often being taught by teachers who are underqualified (Education Trust 2008).

The vision set forth for high school mathematics in this publication depends on teachers who have strong knowledge of mathematical content. Without this knowledge and the confidence it inspires, teachers have difficulty pushing reasoning to the forefront of the curriculum. In essence, more money, resources, and better teachers are being provided to the students who come from the wealthiest families, whereas less money, fewer resources, and less-qualified teachers are provided for the students from the poorest families (Darling-Hammond 2004). Simply providing equitable resources for all students is certainly not sufficient to ensure that each student will develop reasoning and sense making in mathematics, but it is surely necessary for real progress to be made (Bishop and Forgasz 2006). Therefore, attention must be paid to such economic disparities, including attention to the distribution of high-quality teachers, if education is to improve for all students in the United States.

A positive trend is that more African American, Hispanic, and Native American students are studying more advanced mathematics than in previous decades. However, persistent gaps in course taking remain between these students and their white and Asian/Pacific Islander peers. In 2004 approximately 6 percent each of African American, Hispanic, and Native American high school students graduated having completed calculus, as compared with 33 percent of Asian/Pacific Islanders and 16 percent of white students (Planty, Provasnik, and Daniel 2007). The notion that African American, Hispanic, and Native American students are not as interested in or do not value taking advanced mathematics courses as much as their white peers is simply not true. Studies have shown that especially African American and Hispanic students "sometimes have more positive attitudes towards mathematics and higher educational aspirations" (Walker 2007, p. 48) than do their white peers, particularly in the early years of high school. Yet the disparities still exist, often tied to discrepancies in resources, which can have important consequences for students' achievement in mathematics. Hoffer, Rasinski, and Moore (1995), as cited in Tate and Rousseau (2002), found that when African American students and white students completed the same mathematics courses, they had comparable achievement gains. Tate and Rousseau go on to state, "These findings suggest that [many] of racial and SES differences in mathematics achievement in grades 9 through 12 are a product of the quality and the number of mathematics courses that African American, White, Hispanic, high- and low-SES students complete during high secondary school" (p. 276). This powerful finding makes clear the need for high schools to be diligent in supporting all students, especially those students who are often underrepresented in high-level mathematics classes, to study more advanced mathematics.

For more students from all racial and ethnic groups and socioeconomic levels to study more advanced mathematics, they must have the opportunity to enroll in these courses in their high school career. According to the Educational Testing Service (1999), schools having a majority of low-SES students offer fewer advanced mathematics courses than wealthier schools. This outcome, too, is closely connected with a lack of resources—most important, teachers who are qualified to teach advanced mathematics. Failure to offer advanced mathematics courses not only does a great disservice to the students but also perpetuates the shortage of people prepared to enter fields in science, technology, engineering, and mathematics.

Encouraging all students to take advanced mathematics courses is crucial. Walker (2007) offers suggestions that include (1) providing enrichment opportunities so that all students, but especially students from groups less represented in the mathematics pipeline, see mathematics as relevant to future careers and their lives; (2) involving families and communities; and (3) in schools that are less diverse, providing opportunities for engaging in mathematics in diverse student groups. As always, teachers play a crucial role in ensuring that once students are enrolled in advanced courses, those students are able to succeed. Teacher educators and staff developers must assist teachers in learning how to support mathematical reasoning in students who require additional support. For example, teachers can support the development of mathematical reasoning in English Language Learners (ELLs) by encouraging them to discuss their mathematical thinking on a daily basis and by providing them with various opportunities to communicate mathematically. Mathematical activity in which students are asked to reason is a vehicle for enhancing the linguistic skills of students who lack English vocabulary, thus avoiding their placement in remedial mathematics classes and preventing the delay of reasoning activities in the mathematics classroom until they have mastered basic linguistic skills (Moschkovich 2007). Instruction that centers on promoting group interaction, integrates language, uses multiple representations, and emphasizes context is important for the success of ELLs (Bay-Williams and Herrera 2007).

High Expectations

In *Principles and Standards for School Mathematics* (NCTM 2000a), the Equity Principle describes the importance of teachers' holding high expectations for all students. Teachers can motivate their students to perform at high levels by having and communicating high expectations, just as they can lower students' confidence in their mathematical abilities by exhibiting low expectations. Teachers' self-awareness of personal bias about who can and cannot do mathematics is an essential part of holding high expectations for all students. All too often, teachers' and administrators' views of students' ability, motivation, behavior, and future aspirations are influenced by their beliefs associated with such student identifiers as race, gender, socioeconomic status, native language, and home life. In turn, those beliefs can have serious consequences for the opportunities that a school provides to its students. By working to become aware of subconscious attitudes, teachers and administrators can strive to overcome those notions and act purposefully against social inequalities.

Although holding high expectations for all students is crucial, expectations alone are not enough. By taking specific action in the classroom, teachers can truly support students in meeting those high expectations. One such action is to encourage all students to share their thinking and listen to the thinking of others. Establishing a community of learning in which a multitude of approaches and solutions are encouraged and respected is a way to effect positive change (NCTM 2008). Using tasks with multiple entry points is one way to encourage this student interaction, as all students can make a meaningful contribution to the class discussion. Subtle teacher behaviors also demonstrate the belief that all students can be successful. For example, Cousins-Cooper (2000) suggested that teachers can encourage African American students when they get stuck on a problem by asking probing questions instead of showing the students how to do the problem; such behavior is important for teachers of all students. This behavior communicates to the students and all who observe the interaction that the teacher believes that her or his students can be successful in making sense of the problem and working toward a solution. Teachers must be constantly aware of the messages they communicate to students both verbally and nonverbally.

Creating an inclusive environment in which all students—regardless of race, gender, socioeconomic status, or perceived motivation and learning ability—are engaged in reasoning and sense-making activities communicates to students a belief that everyone is expected to be successful in mathematics. Researchers have noted a tremendous difference in success rates among high-minority, low-socioeconomic student populations when a culture of high expectations and a shared goal of success for all students is adopted not just by individual teachers but by the entire school, including families and the community (Gutierrez 2000; Education Trust 2005).

Conclusion

In general, teachers and schools across North America are working tirelessly toward the goal of providing high-quality education to every student in their classrooms. However, in the shuffle of high school life, some students are inadvertently overlooked or underserved. Moreover, the same students are frequently among those overlooked—those of color, those of low or exceptionally high achievement, and those of low socioeconomic status. Teachers, teacher leaders, and administrators, along with families and the community, must constantly reflect on how educational policy and practices may work to support or fail to support giving all students the opportunities with reasoning and sense making that they need to be successful as they exit high school. Some questions to reflect on in trying to reach this goal include these: Are the students enrolled in advanced mathematics courses at a school representative of the demographics of the school? If a school employs tracking, do students move between tracks flexibly and with the support of teachers and administrators? Are decisions on course placements based on evidence rather than subjective judgments that may unintentionally reinforce group stereotypes? In any given mathematics course, are students engaged in reasoning and sense making on a daily basis?

Chapter 10

Coherence

*Curriculum, instruction, and assessment form a
coherent whole to support reasoning
and sense making.*

TO ACHIEVE the vision set forth in this publication, the components of the educational system must work together for the good of the students served by the system. Curriculum, instruction, and assessment can be designed to support students' reasoning and sense making. A coherent and cohesive mathematics program requires strong alignment of these three elements.

Curriculum and Instruction

Increasingly, calls are being made for consistency in the high school mathematics curriculum across the United States (National Science Board 2007). Several sets of recommendations propose a list of content topics delineated by grade level, reflecting a range of goals and priorities (American Diploma Project 2004; College Board 2006, 2007; ACT 2007; Achieve 2007a, 2007b; Franklin et al. 2007). This publication calls for a different type of consistency across the curriculum—curricular emphases and instructional approaches that make reasoning and sense making foundational to the content that is taught and learned. Along with the more-detailed content recommendations outlined in *Principles and Standards* (NCTM 2000a), this publication provides a critical filter in examining any curriculum arrangement to ensure that the ultimate goals of the high school mathematics program are achieved.

Classrooms that promote the goals of this publication prepare students to view mathematics as a connected whole across mathematical domains that consistently involves reasoning and sense making. Fostering depth of students' mathematical knowledge requires classrooms in which students are actively involved in solving problems that require them to make connections among content areas and to develop mathematical reasoning habits. The selection of mathematical tasks to use in instruction is central in promoting reasoning and sense making. Consider some of the qualities of the tasks given in the examples of this publication, including whether they—

- promote sound and significant mathematical content;
- reflect students' understandings, interests, and experiences;
- support the range of ways that diverse students learn mathematics;
- engage students' intellect by requiring reasoning and problem solving;
- help students build connections; and
- promote communication (cf. NCTM [1991]).

Without engaging tasks, teachers' efforts to promote students' reasoning will be limited, no matter how skilled their efforts. The approach common in the United States for many years (Martin 2007), in which teachers introduce a new topic, work out several examples, and then ask their students to emulate what they have seen, will not achieve the goal. A more profitable approach may be "teaching via problem solving" (Schroder and Lester 1989), in which teachers use engaging tasks to help students reason about, and make sense of, new mathematical ideas.

As stated in the Curriculum Principle, "a curriculum is more than a collection of activities: it must be coherent, focused on important mathematics ..." (NCTM 2000a, p. 14). Careful attention must be given to developing sequences of tasks that help students learn important mathematics. Integrated curricula are particularly well suited to meet this goal because they are designed to emphasize connections across mathematical domains. Regardless of the way a curriculum is organized, those involved in the mathematics program must do their best to ensure that all students are being given a strong preparation in mathematics that emphasizes the curricular connections needed to support effective mathematical reasoning and sense making.

Merely creating an organization of worthwhile mathematical tasks within a coherent curriculum is clearly not enough. The tasks must be carried out in a classroom in which a teacher has built a classroom culture that values students' reasoning and sense making. Effective instruction requires having and communicating high expectations for all students. In such learning environments, students continually explore interesting tasks, either individually or in groups, and communicate their conjectures and conclusions to others. Pedagogical techniques and carefully designed instructional materials further ensure that the focus of instruction is on *students'* thinking and reasoning, and provide opportunities for all students to participate. Professional development is necessary to ensure that teachers have the tools they need to build such a classroom culture. See "Developing Reasoning Habits in the Classroom" in chapter 2 for additional commentary on teaching practices that may help develop reasoning and sense making.

Vertical Alignment of Curriculum

All too often students experience discontinuities as they move from one level of mathematics to another (Smith et al. 2000), from middle school to high school and from high school to postsecondary education. The alignment of mathematical expectations related to the goals of this publication is important as students move from one school level to another. To achieve the goal of curricular coherence, an open dialogue is essential among prekindergarten through grade 8 teachers, high school mathematics teachers, mathematics teacher educators, and mathematics and statistics faculty in higher education, as well as from client disciplines, to ensure continuing support and development of students' mathematical abilities.

Schools, families, policymakers, and others need to see evidence that reasoning and sense-making abilities are shared goals among all levels of mathematics teaching, including elementary school mathematics, high school mathematics, and the undergraduate curriculum. The time is right to build strong partnerships among the various constituencies, and to recognize the potential beneficial consequences resulting from a mathematics curriculum that focuses on reasoning and sense making as articulated parts of the continuum from prekindergarten through grade 16.

Alignment with prekindergarten through grade 8 mathematics

This publication takes the recommendations of *Curriculum Focal Points for Prekindergarten through Grade 8 Mathematics* (*Curriculum Focal Points*) (NCTM 2006a) as its starting point for ensuring that proper alignment occurs between the middle grades and high school. For each grade level, prekindergarten through grade 8, *Curriculum Focal Points* outlines Focal Point content areas and describes objectives in additional areas of "related connections." Each chapter of *Curriculum Focal Points* begins with two reminders:

- The "curriculum focal points and related connections … are the recommended content emphases for mathematics…." That is, the objectives outlined in the additional "related connections" are also required material. Otherwise, students will not receive the breadth of mathematical content required for high school, particularly in the areas of data analysis, probability, and statistics.

- "It is essential that these focal points be addressed in contexts that promote problem solving, reasoning, communication, making connections, and designing and analyzing representations." That is, teaching skills without providing a foundation in, and without giving attention to, important mathematical processes, including reasoning and sense making, will not adequately prepare students for the kinds of thinking expected in high school mathematics.

All students entering high school should have a sound base of mathematical experiences as described in the broadest interpretation of *Curriculum Focal Points*.

Taking algebra in middle grades has become increasingly popular (National Center for Educational Statistics 2009). This publication contends that whenever new content is encountered—in elementary, middle, or high school—the foundation for conceptual understanding is laid, in part, through opportunities for students to reason with and about the mathematics being studied and to connect it with their prior knowledge. Therefore, middle school courses that contain significant algebraic content must build on and foster students' reasoning and sense making—including making connections across various mathematical domains—to lay a foundation for success in later courses. For students without the content background described in *Curriculum Focal Points* and with insufficient experience in reasoning and sense making, taking a formal algebra course prematurely will result in missed opportunities for broadening and strengthening their understanding of fundamental mathematical concepts, including those that are foundational for later success in algebra. Taking a formal algebra course too early will be counterproductive unless students have the necessary prerequisite skills because "exposing students to such coursework before they are ready often leads to frustration, failure, and negative attitudes toward mathematics and learning" (NCTM 2008).

Alignment with postsecondary education

Principles and Standards (NCTM 2000a) states, "All students are expected to study mathematics each of the four years that they are enrolled in high school" (p. 288), and students must experience reasoning and sense making across all four years of a high-quality high school mathematics program. This expectation is reinforced in NCTM's (2006b) Position Statement on Time: "Evidence supports the enrollment of high school students in a mathematics course every year, continuing beyond the equivalent of a second year of algebra and a year of geometry."

However, what courses to offer students who have taken formal algebra (and perhaps even geometry) in middle school has become increasingly problematic. If students take calculus in high school, they should take rigorous courses following the Advanced Placement guidelines (College Board 2008a) so that they are prepared to continue their study of mathematics at the collegiate level. Advanced Placement Statistics has become increasingly popular (College Board 2008b) and will meet the needs of many students going on to either mathematics-related or non-mathematics-related majors in college. Developing alternative courses that meet the needs of other students should also be considered—for example, capstone courses are being developed to help students connect what they have been learning with their future goals (cf. Charles A. Dana Center 2008). All upper-level courses should continue to promote the goals of reasoning and sense making as set forth in this publication.

The recommendations in this publication are consistent with recommendations by the Mathematics Association of America (Ganter and Barker 2004, the Committee on the Undergraduate Program in Mathematics [CUPM] 2004), and the American Mathematical Association of Two-Year Colleges (2006). These organizations propose that the entire college-level mathematics curriculum, for all students, even those who take just one course, should develop "analytical, critical reasoning, problem-solving, and communication skills…" (CUPM 2004, pp. 5, 13). The commonalities between recommendations for the undergraduate curriculum and those of the current publication provide opportunities to strengthen articulation between high school and postsecondary education. Furthermore, the framers of this publication believe that focusing on reasoning and sense making can move us forward on important issues, such as those involving mathematics placement examinations used by postsecondary institutions and articulation on the role of technology in high school and college mathematics.

Assessment

What we assess should reflect what we value. Assessments that support the goals of this publication will attend to students' capabilities in mathematical reasoning and sense making and contribute to students' progress in mathematics. This endeavor is essential for at least two reasons. First, we will not be able to gauge whether we are meeting our goals if those goals are not assessed. Second, high-stakes testing that concentrates primarily on procedural skills *without* assessing reasoning and sense making sends a message that is contrary to the vision set forth in this publication and can adversely influence instruction and students' learning. Assessment that focuses primarily on students' ability to do algebraic manipulations, apply geometric formulas, and perform basic statistical computations will lead students to believe that reasoning and sense making are not important.

Assessing students' progress in mathematics serves two distinct roles. One essential role of assessment is to provide summative measures of students' understanding of and ability to use mathematics. All too often, high-stakes tests assess minimal standards that do not reflect the content that students need for their future success. As students, educators, and the community focus on students' success in learning lower-level content, the importance of pushing students to succeed with higher-level content may be diminished. Moreover, this publication calls for further progress in the design of many high-stakes test items to better assess students' reasoning and sense making.

The second essential component of assessment is formative assessment, which is an integral part of the learning process for the student. According to Black and Wiliam (1998), formative assessment involves providing students with learning activities and, on the basis of feedback from those activities, adjusting teaching to meet the students' needs. Various forms of formative assessment can furnish information about students' reasoning and sense making. These include teacher observations, classroom discussions, student journals, student presentations, homework, and in-class tasks, as well as tests and quizzes that ask students to explain their thinking. To ensure that their assessments reflect curricular priorities, teachers must use both summative and formative instruments for assessing students' understanding of mathematics. Example 3, "Around Pi," illustrates the use of an in-class assignment for formative assessment. Regardless of whether a grade is assigned, the teacher might design a rubric, such as that in figure 10.1, to better understand the students' progress in understanding error and relative error.

4	Uses the concept of relative error to establish an upper bound for the error through a clear argument with minimal gaps. Provides an example that reflects the argument.
3	Uses the concept of relative error to establish an upper bound for the error but provides an argument with one or more gaps, or the example does not reflect the argument.
2	Shows some understanding of relative error but is unable to establish an upper bound for the error.
1	Shows limited understanding of relative error.

Fig. 10.1. A rubric for assessing responses to example 3

Conclusion

Alignment of curriculum, instruction, and assessment is a starting point on the road to implementing the goals set forth in this publication within the large and complex educational system of the United States. These three components cannot be viewed in isolation. Rather, decision makers or policymakers dealing with aspects of any one of these areas must ask themselves, "Is a coherent mathematics program being developed that takes into account all three programmatic elements?"

Efforts to focus the mathematics curriculum on reasoning and sense making will require responsible efforts of, and considerable work from, all stakeholders. Support will be required through governing policy statements that clearly align with the goals set forth here. The realization of these recommendations will require considerable time and resources to provide the significant professional development required for school faculty and administrators. Many of these efforts are discussed further in the next chapter.

Chapter 11

Stakeholder Involvement

Everyone involved must work together to ensure that reasoning and sense making are central foci of high school mathematics programs.

THIS publication sets forth an ambitious vision for the improvement of high school mathematics by refocusing it on reasoning and sense making. This refocusing is not a minor tweaking of the system but a substantial rethinking of the high school mathematics curriculum that requires the engagement of all involved in high school mathematics. Significant effort will be needed to realign the curriculum to focus on reasoning and sense making, to provide teachers with the professional development needed to develop new understanding of the curriculum, and to ensure that all students are given the resources needed to prepare them for our rapidly changing world.

The following sections outline questions that decision makers can ask themselves or others as they work with different stakeholder groups to increase their engagement in improving high school mathematics. These questions are intended to form the basis for extended reflection on what is currently happening and what needs to happen, and to spur all involved to begin moving toward the goals of this publication.

Students

- Why is the study of mathematics important for high school students?
    - Do students see mathematics as a useful, interesting, and creative area of study?
    - Do they consider an understanding of mathematics to be an important tool for their future success?
    - Are they taking as much mathematics as possible so that they will have a firm foundation for their future career or further study?

- What do reasoning and sense making mean to high school students?
    - Are they actively working to make sense of the mathematics they are learning?
    - Are they developing the reasoning that underlies mathematical procedures?

- Do high school students work on their mathematics (in class and at home) thoughtfully?
  - Do they look for relationships and connections, both within mathematics and with other areas of inquiry—including other subjects and cocurricular activities?
  - Do they use mathematical procedures in a mindful way that conveys their understanding of them?
  - Do they work at effectively communicating their mathematical reasoning to their classmates and others?

- Do they exhibit a productive attitude toward mathematics and its importance in making decisions about parts of their life outside of school?

Families

- Why should families consider mathematics important for their high school students?
  - Why is a broad preparation in mathematics important?

- What is meant by reasoning and sense making?
  - Will their students learn the skills they need for future success?
  - Will their students be prepared for success in college?

- Do some students possess a "mathematics gene," or can all students be successful in learning to reason mathematically?

- What courses should families ensure that their students are taking so that their students will receive high-quality preparation in mathematics?

- What should families look for in their students' classroom?
  - What kind of homework should their students be given?
  - What kinds of tests should their students take?

- How can families best help their students study mathematics?
  - Are families encouraging their students to work for true understanding rather than just for completion of homework assignments?
  - Are families reinforcing the importance of persistence, even in the face of frustration?

- What are the most important things that families should do to support the mathematics learning of their high school student?
  - Are families encouraging their students to challenge themselves academically?
  - Are families communicating that school should be their students' top priority?

- What should family members do if their child shows mathematical talent?

Teachers

- Are reasoning and sense making the foci of high school mathematics teachers' instruction every day and for every topic within every course?

- Do teachers realize and demonstrate the importance of mathematics reasoning habits and content knowledge as life skills that will ensure their students' success in the future, not just as the prerequisite for the next mathematics course that their students may take?
    — Do teachers help their students see the wide range of careers that involve mathematics—for example, finance, real estate, marketing, advertising, forensics, and even sports journalism?
    — Do teachers emphasize the practical worth of mathematics for addressing real problems and seek contexts in which mathematics can be seen as a useful and important tool for making decisions?

- Do teachers see mathematics as a coherent subject in which the reasons that results are true are as important as the results themselves?

- Do teachers help students make sense of the mathematics for themselves?

- Do teachers help students develop a productive disposition toward mathematics?

- Do teachers strive for balance among the areas of the high school mathematics curriculum outlined in section 2 of this publication and help students find the connections among those areas?

- Do teachers incorporate technology in ways that enhance students' reasoning and sense making?

- Do teachers use a range of assessments to monitor and promote reasoning and sense making, both in identifying students' progress and in making instructional decisions?

- Do teachers recognize the importance of immediately beginning to focus their content and instruction on reasoning and sense making while working with administrators and policymakers toward broadly restructuring the high school mathematics program?

- Do teachers believe that all students are capable of, and can benefit from a focus on, reasoning and sense making, and are they providing the necessary support for students who need extra support?
    — Do teachers ensure that students at all levels have mathematics experiences that are focused on reasoning and sense making?
    — Are teachers advocates for their students, ensuring that schools offer all students the courses that are crucial for their mathematical success?

- Do teachers seek out professional development opportunities that will help them gain a better understanding of the reasoning behind mathematical concepts and ways to develop mathematical reasoning in their students?

Administrators

- Do school districts, schools, departments, and teachers ensure that students receive a high-quality high school mathematics curriculum that promotes reasoning and sense making?

- Do school districts support teachers through long-term professional development that includes reflection on their practice and their work to improve it?

  — Do professional development activities help teachers experience mathematics as reasoning and sense making for themselves?

  — Are teachers given time to collaborate during the school day to improve mathematics instruction—with colleagues teaching at the same level to develop tasks that promote reasoning and sense making and with those teaching at higher and lower levels to ensure that reasoning and sense making are being developed across the grades?

  — Do teachers collaboratively analyze students' work and improve the level of formative feedback for students on reasoning and sense making?

  — Is mentoring provided for novice teachers as they work to develop students' reasoning and sense-making skills?

- Do schools and school districts work with universities, including mathematicians, statisticians, and mathematics teacher educators, to develop effective programs and courses that address teachers' needs?

- Do administrators' classroom observations of mathematics teachers focus on reasoning and sense making and provide useful formative feedback?

- Are support systems in place to provide high school students with the needed assistance to attain high expectations in mathematics?

  — Does the school district's counseling infrastructure promote perseverance in taking higher-level mathematics, thereby supporting the goal of increasing students' mathematical reasoning and sense making?

Policymakers

- Why is mathematics important for high school students?

- Why is high school mathematics education important to the economic competitiveness of the United States in the global marketplace?

- What is meant by reasoning and sense making in mathematics, and why should these outcomes be crucial foci in high school?

- Are reasoning and sense making inextricably integrated with content topics in state and district frameworks that guide curricular decisions?

- Do state and local assessment policies emphasize the need for, and importance of, items that examine students' ability to reason and make sense of mathematical situations?

- How can policymakers help ensure that all students have access to a rich mathematics curriculum based on reasoning and sense making?

- Are adequate resources allocated to assist schools and districts in efforts to effectively implement a curriculum based on reasoning and sense making?

Higher Education

- Do colleges follow the recommendations of the *CUPM Curriculum Guide* (CUPM 2004), which suggests a "move towards reasoning" as the basis for undergraduate mathematics?

- Do college entrance or placement examinations test students' ability to reason mathematically, as well as their ability to carry out mathematical procedures?

- Do mathematics departments act on the recommendations of the *Mathematical Education of Teachers* report (Conference Board of the Mathematical Sciences 2001) for the preparation of high school mathematics teachers?
    - In particular, do they provide "an opportunity for prospective teachers to look deeply at fundamental ideas, to connect topics that often seem unrelated, and to further develop the habits of mind that define mathematical approaches to problems" (p. 46)?
    - Do they provide courses in statistics and probability for prospective high school teachers that emphasize a data-driven and concept-oriented approach?
    - Do prospective and practicing teachers experience reasoning and sense making in all the major areas of mathematics outlined in the report?

- Do colleges of education provide prospective and practicing teachers with courses that emphasize organizing the high school curriculum around reasoning and sense making and instructional methods that support students' development of reasoning and sense making?

- Do mathematicians, statisticians, and mathematics educators collaborate with one another and with K–12 educators to promote reasoning and sense making in high school mathematics?
    - Do they collaborate to develop courses and programs that will support the continued learning of high school teachers as they work to increase the focus in their instruction on reasoning and sense making?
    - Do they seek opportunities to work with K–12 educators in establishing curricular priorities that ensure a balance of content, and in developing state and local curriculum guides and assessment programs that emphasize reasoning and sense making in high school mathematics?

Curriculum Designers

- Do curriculum materials for high school mathematics include a central, regular focus on students' reasoning and sense making that goes beyond the inclusion of isolated supplementary lessons or problems?

- Does the curriculum, whether integrated or following the course sequence customary in the United States, develop connections among content areas so that students see mathematics as a coherent whole?

- Is a balance maintained in the areas of mathematics addressed, so that statistics, for example, is more than an isolated unit?

- Does the curriculum emphasize coherence from one course to the next, demonstrating growth in both mathematical content and reasoning?

- Does the curriculum incorporate technology in ways that enhance students' mathematical understanding?

- Is the design of the curriculum materials based on knowledge about how to support the learning of all students?

Collaboration among Stakeholders

- Are lines of communication among stakeholders being established to promote mathematical reasoning and sense making as central goals of high school mathematics?

- Is collaboration among stakeholders a central feature of efforts to improve the high school mathematics program?

- Is the importance of developing "learning communities" that collaboratively seek continuing improvement across the educational system recognized?

- Is each group of stakeholders identifying both long- and short-term action plans in consultation with other stakeholders and beginning to implement those plans?

Conclusion

This publication demonstrates that all high school mathematics programs need to be focused on providing all students with the mathematical reasoning and sense-making skills necessary for success in their lives within the context of rich content knowledge. The need to refocus the high school mathematics curriculum has been evident for many years (National Commission on Excellence in Education 1983; Mathematical Sciences Education Board 1989; National Commission on Mathematics and Science Teaching for the 21st Century 2000) and has been reflected in the policies and priorities of the National Council of Teachers of Mathematics for nearly thirty years, from *An Agenda for Action* (1980), to *Curriculum and Evaluation Standards for*

School Mathematics (1989), through *Principles and Standards for School Mathematics* (2000a). Although many high school mathematics programs have made significant progress toward achieving such a refocusing, significant work remains to be done to make the deep-rooted, nationwide changes that are vital in meeting the mathematical needs of all students.

Through this publication, NCTM is providing a framework for thinking about the changes that must be made and for beginning to consider how those changes might be accomplished. However, many issues extending beyond what could be addressed in this publication remain to be answered. Over the coming years, NCTM will continue to provide resources and initiatives that build on this framework. One of NCTM's initial efforts is a set of topic books that set forth additional guidance in particular content areas. Subsequent volumes may address additional issues, such as ensuring equitable experiences for all students in reasoning and sense making. NCTM will also seek to partner with other organizations concerned with high school mathematics.

Although NCTM can take a leadership role, all stakeholders must join forces and work together in meaningful ways to ensure that the continuing story of missed opportunities to significantly improve high school mathematics across the United States will not be told five years from now, let alone in three decades. We simply cannot afford to wait any longer to address the large-scale changes that are needed. The success of our students and of our nation depends on it.

Annotated Bibliography

In this section, several citations from each chapter of the publication have been summarized to provide additional insights into, and support for, the ideas discussed.

Chapter 1: Reasoning and Sense Making

1. American Diploma Project. *Ready or Not: Creating a High School Diploma That Counts.* Washington, D.C.: Achieve, 2004.

This report strives to strengthen the connection between high school mathematics and English curricula and the skills and knowledge that high school graduates will need for either college or post-secondary work. Working closely with leaders of higher education as well as workforce leaders, the American Diploma Project describes in this report what students need to know on high school graduation so that they can be successful. Mathematical reasoning is highlighted as important for high school students because both in the workplace and in high school they will be called on to apply mathematical concepts from the classroom to new problems and situations.

2. Kilpatrick, Jeremy, Jane Swafford, and Bradford Findell, eds. *Adding It Up: Helping Children Learn Mathematics.* Washington, D.C.: National Academy Press, 2001.

This National Research Council report synthesizes research and makes recommendations for the teaching and learning of mathematics for kindergarten through eighth-grade students. The report puts forth a model for describing mathematical proficiency that includes conceptual understanding, procedural fluency, strategic competence, adaptive reasoning, and productive disposition. The report describes how each of the five "strands" is a crucial component of students' success in school mathematics.

3. Knuth, Eric J. "Teachers' Conceptions of Proof in the Context of Secondary School Mathematics." *Journal of Mathematics Teacher Education* 5, no. 1 (2002): 61–88.

In this study looking at secondary school mathematics teachers' conception of proof, Knuth presents a framework for understanding the role of proof in school mathematics. This framework draws on other research and provides a useful way of thinking about the purposes of proof in mathematics curricula. In terms of Knuth's framework, proof is a mechanism for verifying and explaining true statements, communicating mathematically, creating and discovering new mathematics, and organizing ideas so that they are part of a structure of axioms.

4. Yackel, Erna, and Gila Hanna. "Reasoning and Proof." In *A Research Companion to "Principles and Standards for School Mathematics,"* edited by Jeremy Kilpatrick, W. Gary Martin, and Deborah Shifter, pp. 227–36. Reston, Va.: National Council of Teachers of Mathematics, 2003.

This chapter highlights research on reasoning and proof in K–12 education. The authors report research that supports the importance of reasoning in students' learning of mathematics. Further, they discuss the crucial role of proof in the field of mathematics and consequently in K–12 mathematics. Proof is more than just a means of verification of a statement; it also serves as a vehicle for explanation and systemization of observed relationships and patterns.

Chapter 2: Reasoning Habits

1. Cuoco, Al, E. Paul Goldenberg, and June Mark. "Habits of Mind: An Organizing Principle for Mathematics Curriculum." *Journal of Mathematical Behavior* 15 (December 1996): 375–402.

The authors make the case for emphasizing more than just mathematical content in high school mathematics. They propose that high school students need to develop mathematical habits of mind. These ways of thinking about mathematics, modeled after the work of mathematicians, will continue to be relevant to students even as content changes over time. The article describes in detail the habits of mind that high school students should be developing as part of their mathematics experience.

2. Committee on the Undergraduate Program in Mathematics of the Mathematical Association of America (CUPM). *Undergraduate Programs and Courses in the Mathematical Sciences: CUPM Curriculum Guide 2004.* Washington, D.C.: Mathematical Association of America, 2004.

The CUPM of the Mathematical Association of America is charged with making recommendations to colleges and universities about undergraduate mathematics education. Every ten years, on the basis of consultations with mathematicians and representatives from related disciplines, the committee updates and makes available the list of recommendations. Among other recommendations, the report points to the need for every undergraduate mathematics course to develop critical reasoning and mathematical habits of mind in students.

3. Garfield, Joan. "The Challenge of Developing Statistical Reasoning." *Journal of Statistics Education* 10, no. 3 (2002). http://www.amstat.org/publications/jse/v10n3/garfield.html.

The author defines and discusses research on statistical reasoning. She also describes a developmental model portraying five stages of statistical reasoning for students. In addition, she considers implications for assessment and teaching.

4. Harel, Guershon, and Larry Sowder. "Advanced Mathematical-Thinking at Any Age: Its Nature and Its Development." *Mathematical Thinking and Learning* 7, no. 1 (2005): 27–50.

This article makes the case that advanced mathematical thinking is not just mathematical thinking about advanced mathematics but advanced thinking about mathematics that can occur as early as in elementary school. Students have many important opportunities to develop such ways of thinking in elementary and secondary school mathematics. The authors also describe hindrances, including particular instructional practices, to students developing advanced mathematical thinking.

Chapter 4: Reasoning with Number and Measurement

1. Carraher, David W., and Analucia D. Schliemann, "Early Algebra and Algebraic Reasoning." In *Second Handbook of Research on Mathematics Teaching and Learning,* edited by Frank K. Lester, pp. 669–705. Charlotte, N.C.: Information Age Publishing; Reston, Va.: National Council of Teachers of Mathematics, 2007.

This review of literature on early algebraic learning and reasoning discusses the important relationship between arithmetic and elementary algebra. Findings in the reviewed research include the implication that arithmetic can be viewed as a part of algebra as opposed to a separate entity and as such is promising as an entry point into learning algebra. In particular, understanding the structure of numbers, such as numerical properties, may prevent some common misunderstandings in algebra on the part of students.

2. Lehrer, Richard. "Developing Understanding of Measurement." In *A Research Companion to "Principles and Standards for School Mathematics,"* edited by Jeremy Kilpatrick, W. Gary Martin, and Deborah Schifter, pp. 179–92. Reston, Va.: National Council of Teachers of Mathematics, 2003.

In this survey of research on measurement, the author discusses the centrality of error to measure and approximation. Although much of the research described deals with younger children, it supports the importance of giving students opportunities in the classroom to struggle with and understand error.

3. Sowder, Judith. "Estimation and Number Sense." In *Handbook of Research on Mathematics Teaching and Learning,* edited by Douglas A. Grouws, pp. 371–89. Reston, Va.: National Council of Teachers of Mathematics, 1992.

This review of research on mathematical estimation and number sense discusses three related areas: computational estimation, measurement estimation, and number sense. The chapter makes a case for the importance of both school-aged children's and adults' being able to estimate in both in-school and out-of-school contexts. Posessing a deep understanding of number, including understanding magnitude and numerical comparisons, and being about to reason about number are vital to being a good estimator.

4. National Mathematics Advisory Panel. *Foundations for Success: The Final Report of the National Mathematics Advisory Panel.* http://www.ed.gov/about/bdscomm/list/mathpanel/index.html.

The National Mathematics Advisory Panel was formed by presidential order to explore available research on how to improve mathematics performance among American students, particularly focusing on algebra as a gateway to success in mathematics. Among other recommendations in its final report, the panel highlights the importance of number sense for older students as well as younger students. Number-sense concepts, including place value and magnitude of numbers, as well as how these concepts extend beyond whole numbers to numbers expressed as fractions, decimals, and exponents, are crucial for problem solving. In addition, the report emphasizes the importance of fractions in students' success in algebra.

Chapter 5: Reasoning with Algebraic Symbols

1. Fey, James T., ed. *Computing and Mathematics: The Impact on the Secondary School Curricula.* College Park, Md.: University of Maryland, 1984.

This examination of technology in mathematics education from the 1980s includes considerations and comparisons that are still important today. In addition to examining the impact of modern mathematical notation, the authors note that mathematics education influences the discovery of new technology, which in turn influences mathematics education. They describe the history of mathematics education as characterized by cycles of stability and unrest. The editor also notes aspects of the potential impact of technology on curriculum, teaching, and learning.

2. Radford, Luis, and Luis Puig. "Syntax and Meaning as Sensuous, Visual, Historical Forms of Algebraic Thinking." *Educational Studies in Mathematics* 66, no. 2 (October 2007): 145–64.

This article notes that the development of symbolic algebra is considered a great cultural accomplishment. It examines the development of algebraic symbolism from a semiotic viewpoint and observes the effects of culture on both the development of ninth-century Arabic notation and contemporary mathematics students in a modern school setting. The authors highlight some conceptual challenges that can arise in the learning of algebra. One such point is that in learning to understand algebra, students must be able to make some sense of the visual images created by algebraic symbols; doing so may involve understanding multilayered meanings.

3. Saul, Mark. "Algebra: What Are We Teaching?" In *The Roles of Representation in School Mathematics,* 2001 Yearbook of the National Council of Teachers of Mathematics (NCTM), edited by Albert A. Cuoco, pp. 35–43. Reston, Va.: NCTM, 2001.

Saul identifies three levels in learning algebra: generalization of arithmetic, attention to binary operations, and recognition of algebraic form (in which students can conceive of variables as representing complex algebraic expressions). Students with insufficient understanding will cling to memorized rules. Taking away the possibility of trial and error can force students to focus on the operations involved in an algebraic problem and move them from the first level of understanding to the second.

4. Kaput, James J., Maria L. Blanton, and Luis Moreno. "Algebra from a Symbolization Point of View." In *Algebra in the Early Grades,* edited by James J. Kaput, Daniel W. Carraher, and Maria L. Blanton, pp. 19–51. New York: Lawrence Erlbaum Associates, 2008.

This analysis of the process of symbolization as it relates to the development of algebraic understanding notes that symbolization is driven by representational economy and communicative power. Communicative power can be measured in terms of argument and justification. When these processes are not present and "the symbolization process is cut short," algebraic learning difficulties can be expected to arise (p. 46). The topics discussed include the transition from arithmetic to algebra, joint variations and functions, and modeling.

5. Katz, Victor J., and Bill Barton. "Stages in the History of Algebra with Implications for Teaching." *Educational Studies in Mathematics* 66, no. 2 (October 2007): 185–201.

The authors include the geometric stage as one of the conceptual stages of the development of algebraic ideas. They note that an introduction to the idea of function through a geometric tool could be a useful approach and that the idea of function was originally developed through geometry. Other ideas include the remaining three stages of conceptual development: static equation-solving, dynamic function, and abstraction. The authors suggest that because algebra arose from the need to solve problems, a problem-solving approach may help overcome the barrier that algebra often presents.

Chapter 6: Reasoning with Functions

1. Yerushalmy, Michal, and Beba Shternberg. "Charting a Visual Course to the Concept of Function." In *The Roles of Representation in School Mathematics,* 2001 Yearbook of the National Council of Teachers of Mathematics (NCTM), edited by Albert A. Cuoco, pp. 251–67. Reston, Va.: NCTM, 2001.

In making the case for the development and use of technology that helps students build a visual understanding of functions, the researchers show that students with a good concept of function are able to solve real-world problems more easily and identify important properties of mathematical representations of situations. They maintain that introduction to symbolic representations can follow the use of other visual representations of functions. The software that they developed, Function Sketcher, allows students to draw the movements in a real-life situation with freehand mouse movements connected to a Cartesian graph, use iconic graph portions for different types of rates of change (increasing, decreasing, constant), and represent incremental rates of change by using stairstep visuals with graphs.

2. Lloyd, Gwendolyn M., and Marvin (Skip) Wilson. "Supporting Innovation: The Impact of a Teacher's Conceptions of Function on His Implementation of a Reform Curriculum." *Journal for Research in Mathematics Education* 29, no. 3 (May 1998): 248–74.

This examination of the effect of one teacher's conception of function on his teaching contains an introductory discussion of the concept of function that notes the powerful and permeating nature of function in mathematics and its ability to give meaning to complex situations. Among the topics discussed are concept images and the power that comes from understanding multiple representations. Each representational format has different strengths in different situations, so the user needs to have an integrated concept image that allows the knowledgeable choice of which one to use. The teacher's dialogues with students reflect an integrated understanding of the function concept that allows him to use reform-based published materials effectively.

3. Coulombe, Wendy N., and Sarah B. Berenson. "Representations of Patterns and Functions: Tools for Learning." In *The Roles of Representation in School Mathematics,* 2001 Yearbook of the National Council of Teachers of Mathematics (NCTM), edited by Albert A. Cuoco, pp. 166–72. Reston, Va.: NCTM, 2001.

This article contains three examples of functions that address different forms of mathematical knowledge. A weight-loss example addresses graphical interpretation and data generation. An iced-tea example addresses verbal pattern description. An allowance example addresses qualitative graphical construction. The authors emphasize the point that the ability to interpret and translate representations can help students construct mental images of patterns and functions and thus extend their algebraic thinking. A deeper interpretation based on familiar events and problem solving can broaden students' understanding of conventional representations beyond mere manipulation. Furthermore, asking a student to interpret a concept by using a representation different from the one with which it is initially presented is one way to determine students' understanding.

4. Chazan, Daniel, and Michal Yerushalmy. "On Appreciating the Cognitive Complexity of School Algebra: Research on Algebra Learning and Directions of Curricular Change." In *A Research Companion to "Principles and Standards for School Mathematics,"* edited by Jeremy Kilpatrick, W. Gary Martin, and Deborah Schifter, pp. 123–33. Reston, Va.: National Council of Teachers of Mathematics, 2003.

The authors note that learners experience complexities of thought that the traditional focus on solution methods does not directly address. For example, more differences exist among strings of symbols labeled as equations than the standard definition of equations indicates. More specific terminology might label some equations as formulas, open sentences, identities, functions, or properties, depending on the different uses of variables. To address the need that students have for greater understanding of algebraic symbolization, they should work on tasks that can be approached from multiple perspectives. Content should focus on a small set of big ideas, and instruction should connect with students' experiences.

Chapter 7: Reasoning with Geometry

1. Battista, Michael T. "The Development of Geometric and Spatial Thinking." In *Second Handbook of Research on Mathematics Teaching and Learning,* edited by Frank K. Lester, pp. 843–908. Charlotte, N.C.: Information Age Publishing; Reston, Va.: National Council of Teachers of Mathematics, 2007.

In this review of research, the author looks broadly at research on geometric and spatial reasoning. He examines several theories related to students' thinking in geometry and discusses in detail the van Hiele levels, a theory of the way students progress through geometric thinking. The author considers the compelling research supporting these levels of development as informative for understanding students' thinking in geometry.

2. Clements, Douglas. "Teaching and Learning Geometry." In *A Research Companion to "Principles and Standards for School Mathematics,"* edited by Jeremy Kilpatrick, W. Gary Martin, and Deborah Schifter, pp. 151–78. Reston, Va.: National Council of Teachers of Mathematics, 2003.

The author discusses research on teaching and learning geometry. In the United States, as compared with other countries, students have fewer meaningful opportunities to study geometry throughout their K–12 education. Providing opportunities for reasoning with geometry at earlier grades would allow high school students' experiences with geometry to be more profound. A discussion of theories of geometrical thinking, research on using technology in geometry, and implications for teaching and curricular practices are included.

3. Herbst, Patricio G. "Engaging Students in Proving: A Double Bind on the Teacher." *Journal for Research in Mathematics Education* 33 (May 2002): 176–203.

The author uses data from a high school mathematics classroom to discuss the impact of the traditional, formal two-column proof on the teacher. In particular, he describes a struggle between competing goals for students—developing the ideas for the proof versus proving a proposition. He discusses implications for instruction and the role of formal proof in high school mathematics.

Chapter 8: Reasoning with Statistics and Probability

1. Ganter, Susan L., and William Barker, eds. *The Curriculum Foundations Project: Voices of the Partner Disciplines.* Washington, D.C.: Mathematical Association of America, 2004.

This report describes the work of the Mathematical Association of America's Curriculum Foundations Project, in which representatives from college disciplines outside of mathematics met to discuss their students' mathematical needs with representatives from mathematics departments. The result is a common vision for the first two years of undergraduate mathematics. Statistics and data analysis are noted as crucial for students majoring in many of these disciplines and as such are highlighted as an important part of the undergraduate mathematics experience.

2. Franklin, Christine, Gary Kader, Denise Mewborn, Jerry Moreno, Roxy Peck, Mike Perry, and Richard Scheaffer. *Guidelines for Assessment and Instruction in Statistics Education (GAISE) Report: A Pre-K–12 Curriculum Framework.* Alexandria, Va.: American Statistical Association, 2007.

In this framework for the teaching of statistics, leaders in statistics and statistics education make the case for a stronger emphasis on statistics in the K–12 classroom on the basis of the increased necessity for understanding of and the ability to use data. Throughout their school experience, all students should have experiences with, and become proficient in, statistical problem solving. This document fosters greater insight into what these experiences should entail.

3. Kader, Gary, and Jim Mamer. "Statistics in the Middle Grades: Understanding Center and Spread." *Mathematics Teaching in the Middle School* 14 (August 2008): 38–43.

This article, one in a series of articles published for each grade level, is based on the GAISE report of the American Statistical Association (Franklin et al. 2007) and describes the development of basic understanding of the distribution of a data-based variable from elementary to high school. In this article about middle school, the focus is on understanding center and spread. The authors discuss several different mathematical tasks used in classrooms, as well as students' responses.

4. Scheaffer, Richard, and Josh Tabor. "Statistics in the High School Mathematics Curriculum: Building Sound Reasoning under Uncertain Conditions." *Mathematics Teacher* 102 (August 2008): 56–61.

This article, one in a series of articles published for each grade level, is based on the GAISE report of the American Statistical Association (Franklin et al. 2007) and describes the development of basic understanding of the distribution of a data-based variable from elementary to high school. In this article about high school, the focus is on building sound reasoning under conditions of uncertainty.

Chapter 9: Equity

1. Tate, William, and Celia Rousseau. "Access and Opportunity: The Political and Social Context of Mathematics Education." In *Handbook of International Research in Mathematics Education,* edited by Lyn D. English, pp. 271–99. Mahwah, N.J.: Lawrence Erlbaum Associates, 2002.

In this handbook chapter, the authors look at the political, historical, and social context of mathematics education and the resulting impact on equitable access to school mathematics. Discrepancies in course taking, tracking, teacher quality, and equity at the classroom level are discussed as having an impact on differences in learning opportunities for students of color, students in urban schools, and students of low socioeconomic status.

2. Tate, William F., and Celia Rousseau. "Engineering Change in Mathematics Education: Research, Policy, and Practice." In *Second Handbook of Research on Mathematics Teaching and Learning,* edited by Frank K. Lester, pp. 1209–46. Charlotte, N.C: Information Age Publishing; Reston, Va.: National Council of Teachers of Mathematics, 2007.

This chapter provides direction and strategies for teachers, schools, and districts trying to improve mathematics teaching and learning in the No Child Left Behind era. As a result, it discusses the current pressures on schools because of the increased focus on testing. In particular, the authors note that the increased focus on testing is detrimental for all students, but in particular for poor and minority students, whose opportunities for important mathematical reasoning and thinking are limited as a result.

3. Education Trust. *Gaining Traction, Gaining Ground: How Some High Schools Accelerate Learning for Struggling Students.* Washington, D.C.: Education Trust, 2005.

This work is a report of a study comparing seven public high schools—four of which demonstrated incredible growth in students who entered high school significantly behind their peers. These four exemplar schools were compared against high schools that had average growth. The schools all had similar demographics—predominantly minority and low-socioeconomic-status student populations. The study reveals those approaches adopted in the successful schools.

4. Planty, Michael, Stephen Provasnik, and Bruce Daniel. *High School Coursetaking: Findings from the Condition of Education, 2007.* Washington, D.C.: U.S. Department of Education, National Center for Education Statistics, 2007.

This report provides statistics on trends in United States high school course taking from 1982 through 2005. Some of the trends discussed include the coursework offered by different schools, changes in graduation requirements over the past two decades, and the percent of students who take advanced coursework in science and mathematics. The report also compares trends across racial and socioeconomic subgroups.

Chapter 10: Coherence

1. Black, Paul, and Dylan Wiliam. "Inside the Black Box: Raising Standards through Classroom Assessment. *Phi Delta Kappan* 80 (October 1998): 139–44.

This article looks at research to show that formative assessment has a major impact on classroom instruction. Evidence also shows that formative assessment can have a major impact on students' learning. The authors suggest improvements in formative assessment and ways to make those improvements.

2. National Science Board. *A National Action Plan for Addressing the Critical Needs of the U.S. Science, Technology, Engineering, and Mathematics Education System.* Arlington, Va.: National Science Foundation, 2007.

This report calls attention to the need to address issues in STEM (science, technology, engineering, and mathematics) education. The National Science Board makes strong recommendations for alignment within K–12 STEM education and then between K–12 STEM education and STEM higher education and the workforce. Specific recommendations related to this goal of alignment and others are provided.

3. Smith, Jack, Beth Herbel-Eisenmann, Amanda Jansen, and Jon Star. "Studying Mathematical Transitions: How Do Students Navigate Fundamental Changes in Curriculum and Pedagogy?" Paper presented at the 2000 annual meeting of the American Educational Research Association, New Orleans, April 2000.

The authors report on research looking at the impact of transitioning from high school to college and between using traditional curricula and reform curricula. Moving between different curricular approaches is difficult for students because the expectations for learning and doing mathematics are very different with each of these approaches. Students then must then navigate between, in essence, two different mathematical environments.

References

ACT. *ACT National Curriculum Survey,* 2005–2006. Iowa City: ACT, 2007.

Achieve. *High School Model Three-Year Integrated Course Sequence.* American Diploma Project, 2007a. http://www.achieve.org/node/969.

———. *High School Model Three-Year Traditional Plus Course Sequence.* American Diploma Project, 2007b. http://www.achieve.org/node/969.

Alvarez, Doris, and Hugh Mehan. "Whole-School Detracking: A Strategy for Equity and Excellence." *Theory into Practice* 45 (February 2006): 82–89.

American Diploma Project. *Ready or Not: Creating a High School Diploma That Counts.* Washington, D.C.: Achieve, 2004.

American Mathematical Association of Two-Year Colleges (AMATYC). *Beyond Crossroads: Implementing Mathematics Standards in the First Two Years of College.* Memphis, Tenn.: AMATYC, 2006.

Association for Operations Management (APICS). *APICS 2001 International Conference and Exposition Proceedings: San Antonio; Exploring New Frontiers with APICS Education.* CD-ROM. Chicago: APICS, 2001.

Bailey, David H., and Jonathan M. Borwein. "Experimental Mathematics: Examples, Methods and Implications." *Notices of the American Mathematical Society* 52 (May 2005): 502–14.

Baker, Stephen, and Bremen Leak. "Math Will Rock Your World." *Business Week,* January 23, 2006. http://www.businessweek.com/magazine/content/06_04/b3968001.

Battista, Michael T. "The Development of Geometric and Spatial Thinking." In *Second Handbook of Research on Mathematics Teaching and Learning,* edited by Frank K. Lester, pp. 843–908. Charlotte, N.C.: Information Age Publishing; Reston, Va.: National Council of Teachers of Mathematics, 2007.

Bay-Williams, Jennifer M., and Socorro Herrara. "Is 'Just Good Teaching' Enough to Support the Learning of English Language Learners? Insights from Sociocultural Learning Theory." In *The Learning of Mathematics,* 69th Yearbook of the National Council of Teachers of Mathematics (NCTM), edited by Marilyn Strutchens and W. Gary Martin, pp. 43–63. Reston, Va.: NCTM, 2007.

Bishop, Alan, and Helen Forgasz. "Issues in Access and Equity in Mathematics Education." In *Second Handbook of Research on Mathematics Teaching and Learning,* edited by Frank K. Lester, pp. 1145–68. Charlotte, N.C.: Information Age Publishing; Reston, Va.: National Council of Teachers of Mathematics, 2007.

Black, Paul, and Dylan Wiliam. "Inside the Black Box: Raising Standards through Classroom Assessment." *Phi Delta Kappan* 80 (October 1998): 139–44.

Burrill, Gail, Christine A. Franklin, Landy Godbold, and Linda J. Young. *Navigating through Data Analysis in Grades 9–12.* Reston, Va.: National Council of Teachers of Mathematics, 2003.

Carraher, David W., and Analucia D. Shliemann. "Early Algebra and Algebraic Reasoning." In *Second Handbook of Research on Mathematics Teaching and Learning,* edited by Frank K. Lester, pp. 669–705. Charlotte, N.C.: Information Age Publishing; Reston, Va.: National Council of Teachers of Mathematics, 2007.

Chang, Richard S. "The Illusion of Miles per Gallon." *New York Times,* June 20, 2008. http://wheels.blogs.nytimes.com/2008/06/20/the-illusion-of-miles-per-gallon.

Charles A. Dana Center. "Fourth-Year Capstone Courses." Austin, Tex.: University of Texas, 2008. http://www .utdanacenter.org/k12mathbenchmarks/resources/capstone.php.

Chazan, Daniel, and Michal Yerushalmy. "On Appreciating the Cognitive Complexity of School Algebra: Research on Algebra Learning and Directions of Curricular Change." In *A Research Companion to "Principles and Standards for School Mathematics,"* edited by Jeremy Kilpatrick, W. Gary Martin, and Deborah Shifter, pp. 123–33. Reston, Va.: National Council of Teachers of Mathematics, 2003.

Cobb, George W., and David S. Moore. "Mathematics, Statistics, and Teaching." *American Mathematical Monthly* 104 (November 1997): 801–23.

College Board. *College Board Standards for College Success: Mathematics and Statistics.* New York: College Board, 2006.

———. *College Board Standards for College Success: Mathematics and Statistics: Adapted for an Integrated Curricula.* New York: College Board, 2007.

———. *College Board AP Calculus Course Description, May 2009.* New York: College Board, 2008a. http://apcentral.collegeboard.com/apc/public/repository/ap08_calculus_coursedesc.pdf.

———. *The AP Statistics Exam.* New York: College Board, 2008b. http://apcentral.collegeboard.com/apc/members/exam/exam_questions/8357.html

Committee on Science, Engineering, and Public Policy. *Rising above the Gathering Storm: Energizing and Employing America for a Brighter Economic Future.* Washington, D.C.: National Academies Press, 2006.

Committee on the Undergraduate Program in Mathematics of the Mathematical Association of America (CUPM). *Undergraduate Programs and Courses in the Mathematical Sciences: CUPM Curriculum Guide 2004.* Washington, D.C.: Mathematical Association of America, 2004.

Conference Board of the Mathematical Sciences. *The Mathematical Education of Teachers.* Providence, R.I.: American Mathematical Society; Washington, D.C.: Mathematical Association of America, 2001.

Coulombe, Wendy N., and Sarah B. Berenson. "Representations of Patterns and Functions: Tools for Learning." In *The Roles of Representation in School Mathematics,* 2001 Yearbook of the National Council of Teachers of Mathematics (NCTM), edited by Albert A. Cuoco, pp. 166–72. Reston, Va.: NCTM, 2001.

Cousins-Cooper, Kathy M. "Teacher Expectations and Their Effects on African American Students' Success in Mathematics." In *Changing the Faces of Mathematics,* edited by Marilyn E. Strutchens, Martin L. Johnson, and William F. Tate, pp. 15–20. Reston, Va.: National Council of Teachers of Mathematics, 2000.

Coxford, Arthur F., and Zalman P. Usiskin. *Geometry: A Transformation Approach.* River Forest, Ill.: Laidlaw Brothers, 1971.

Cuoco, Al, E. Paul Goldenberg, and June Mark. "Habits of Mind: An Organizing Principle for Mathematics Curriculum." *Journal of Mathematical Behavior* 15 (December 1996): 375–402.

Darling-Hammond, Linda. "The Color Line in American Education: Race, Resources, and Student Achievement." *DuBois Review* 1 (September 2004): 213–46.

Driscoll, Mark J. *Fostering Algebraic Thinking.* Portsmouth, N.H.: Heinemann, 1999.

Education Trust. *Gaining Traction, Gaining Ground: How Some High Schools Accelerate Learning for Struggling Students.* 2005. http://www2.edtrust.org/EdTrust/Product+Catalog/recentreports.

———. *Core Problems: Out-of-Field Teaching Persists in Key Academic Courses and High-Poverty Schools.* 2008. http://www2.edtrust.org/EdTrust/Press+Room/CoreProblems.htm.

Educational Testing Service. "ETS Policy Notes—Opportunity Offered, Opportunity Taken: Course-Taking in American High Schools." 1999. http://www.ets.org/Media/Research/pdf/PICPNV9N1.pdf.

Fey, James T., ed. *Computing and Mathematics: The Impact on the Secondary School Curricula.* College Park: University of Maryland, 1984.

Franklin, Christine, Gary Kader, Denise Mewborn, Jerry Moreno, Roxy Peck, Mike Perry, and Richard Scheaffer. *Guidelines for Assessment and Instruction in Statistics Education (GAISE) Report: A Pre-K–12 Curriculum Framework.* Alexandria, Va.: American Statistical Association, 2007.

Friedman, Thomas L. *The World Is Flat: A Brief History of the Twenty-first Century, Further Updated and Expanded.* New York: Farrar, Straus, and Giroux, 2007.

Ganter, Susan L., and William Barker, eds. *The Curriculum Foundations Project: Voices of the Partner Disciplines.* Washington, D.C.: Mathematical Association of America, 2004.

Garfield, Joan. "The Challenge of Developing Statistical Reasoning." *Journal of Statistics Education* 10, November 2002. http://www.amstat.org/publications/jse/v10n3/garfield.html.

Garrity, Delia. "Detracking with Vigilance." *School Administrator,* 61 (August 2004): 24–27. http://www.aasa.org/publications/saarticledetail.cfm?ItemNumber=1226.

Gutierrez, Rochelle. "Advancing African American Urban Youth in Mathematics: Unpacking the Success of One Math Department." *American Journal of Education* 109 (November 2000): 63–111.

Hallinan, Maureen T. "Whatever Happened to the Detracking Movement?" *Education Next* 4 (Fall 2004): 72–76.

Harel, Guershon, and Larry Sowder. "Advanced Mathematical Thinking at Any Age: Its Nature and Its Development." *Mathematical Thinking and Learning* 7 (January 2005): 27–50.

Herbst, Patricio G. "Engaging Students in Proving: A Double Bind on the Teacher." *Journal for Research in Mathematics Education* 33 (May 2002): 176–203.

Hiebert, James. "What Research Says about the NCTM Standards." In *A Research Companion to "Principles and Standards for School Mathematics,"* edited by Jeremy Kilpatrick, W. Gary Martin, and Deborah Schifter, pp. 5–23. Reston, Va.: National Council of Teachers of Mathematics, 2003.

Hirsch, Christian R., James T. Fey, Eric W. Hart, Harold L. Schoen, and Ann E. Watkins. *Contemporary Mathematics in Context, Course 1.* New York: Glencoe/McGraw Hill, 2007.

Huebner, Tracey A., Grace C. Corbett, and Kate Phillippo. *Rethinking High School: Inaugural Graduations at New York City's New High Schools.* San Francisco: West Ed, 2006.

Kader, Gary, and Jim Mamer. "Statistics in the Middle Grades: Understanding Center and Spread." *Mathematics Teaching in the Middle School* 14 (August 2008): 38–43.

Kaput, James J., Maria L. Blanton, and Luis Moreno. "Algebra from a Symbolization Point of View." In *Algebra in the Early Grades,* edited by James J. Kaput, David W. Carraher, and Maria L. Blanton, pp. 19–51. New York: Lawrence Erlbaum Associates, 2008.

Katz, Victor J. "Stages in the History of Algebra with Implications for Teaching." *Educational Studies in Mathematics* 66 (October 2007): 185–201.

Kilpatrick, Jeremy, Jane Swafford, and Bradford Findell, eds. *Adding It Up: Helping Children Learn Mathematics.* Washington, D.C.: National Academy Press, 2001.

Knuth, Eric. "The Rebirth of Proof in School Mathematics in the United States?" *International Newsletter on the Teaching and Learning of Mathematical Proof,* May/June 2000. http://www.lettredelapreuve.it/Newsletter/000506Theme/000506ThemeUK.html.

Kordemsky, Boris A., and Albert Parry. *The Moscow Puzzles: 359 Mathematical Recreations.* Translated by Albert Parry. Mineola, N.Y.: Dover Publications, 1992.

Lehrer, Richard. "Developing Understanding of Measurement." In *A Research Companion to "Principles and Standards for School Mathematics,"* edited by Jeremy Kilpatrick, W. Gary Martin, and Deborah Shifter, pp. 179–92. Reston, Va.: National Council of Teachers of Mathematics, 2003.

Lloyd, Gwendolyn M., and Melvin Wilson. "Supporting Innovation: The Impact of a Teacher's Conceptions of Function on His Implementation of a Reform Curriculum." *Journal for Research in Mathematics Education* 29 (May 1998): 248–74.

Lubienski, Sarah T., and Michele D. Crockett. "NAEP Findings Regarding Race and Ethnicity: Mathematics Achievement, Student Affect, and School-Home Experiences." In *Results and Interpretations of the 2003 Mathematics Assessment of the National Assessment of Educational Progress,* edited by Peter Kloosterman and Frank K. Lester, pp. 227–60. Reston: Va.: National Council of Teachers of Mathematics, 2007.

Martin, Tami S., ed. *Mathematics Teaching Today: Improving Practice, Improving Student Learning.* 2nd ed. Reston, Va.: National Council of Teachers of Mathematics, 2007.

Martin, W. Gary. *Geometry: A Moving Experience.* Honolulu, Hawaii: Curriculum Research and Development Group, 1996.

Mathematical Sciences Education Board. *Everybody Counts: A Report to the Nation on the Future of Mathematics Education.* Washington, D.C.: National Academy Press, 1989.

Moschkovich, Judit. "Bilingual Mathematics Learners: How Views of Language, Bilingual Learners, and Mathematics Communication Affect Instruction." In *Improving Access to Mathematics—Diversity and Equity in the Classroom,* pp. 89–104. New York: Teachers College, Columbia University, 2007.

National Association for Gifted Children (NAGC). "Differentiation of Curriculum and Instruction." NAGC position statement. 1994. http://www.nagc.org/index.aspx?id=387.

National Center for Education Statistics (NCES). *NAEP Data Explorer,* 2009. http://nces.ed.gov/nationsreportcard/nde/criteria.asp.

National Commission on Excellence in Education. *A Nation at Risk: An Imperative for Educational Reform.* Washington, D.C.: National Commission on Excellence in Education, 1983.

National Commission on Mathematics and Science Teaching for the 21st Century. *Before It's Too Late.* Washington, D.C.: National Commission on Mathematics and Science Teaching for the 21st Century, 2000.

National Council of Teachers of Mathematics (NCTM). *An Agenda for Action.* Reston, Va.: NCTM, 1980.

———. *Curriculum and Evaluation Standards for School Mathematics.* Reston, Va.: NCTM, 1989.

———. *Professional Standards for Teaching Mathematics.* Reston, Va.: NCTM, 1991.

———. *Principles and Standards for School Mathematics.* Reston, Va.: NCTM, 2000a.

———. *Principles and Standards for School Mathematics: E-Standards.* CD-ROM, version 2. Reston, Va.: NCTM, 2000b.

———. *Curriculum Focal Points for Prekindergarten through Grade 8 Mathematics: A Quest for Coherence.* Reston, Va.: NCTM, 2006a.

———. "Math Takes Time." NCTM position statement. 2006b. http://www.nctm.org/about/content.aspx?id=6348.

———. "Equity in Mathematics Education." NCTM position statement. 2008. http://www.nctm.org/about/content.aspx?id=13490.

National Mathematics Advisory Panel. *Foundations for Success: The Final Report of the National Mathematics Advisory Panel.* Washington, D.C.: U.S. Department of Education, 2008.

National Science Board. *A National Action Plan for Addressing the Critical Needs of the U. S. Science, Technology, Engineering, and Mathematics Education System.* Arlington, Va.: National Science Foundation, 2007.

No Child Left Behind Act of 2001. Public Law 107–110. 107th Cong., 1st sess. 8 January 2002.

Partnership for 21st Century Skills. *Beyond the Three Rs: Voter Attitudes toward 21st Century Skills.* Report on results of the nationwide poll, September, 2007. http://www.21stcenturyskills.org/documents/P21_pollreport_singlepg.pdf.

Planty, Michael, Stephen Provasnik, and Bruce Daniel. *High School Coursetaking: Findings from "The Condition of Education 2007"* NCES 2007-065. U.S. Department of Education. Washington, D.C.: National Center for Education Statistics, 2007.

Pollak, Henry. "Why Does a Truck So Often Get Stuck in Our Overpass?" *Consortium: Newsletter of the Consortium for Mathematics and Its Applications* (Spring/Summer 2004): 3–4.

Pólya, George. "On Plausible Reasoning." In *Proceedings of the International Congress of Mathematicians—1950, Vol. 1,* pp. 739–47, Providence, R.I.: American Mathematical Society, 1952.

———. *How to Solve It.* 2nd ed. Princeton, N.J.: Princeton University Press, 1957.

Programme for International Student Assessment (PISA). *PISA 2006: Science Competencies for Tomorrow's World.* Paris: Organisation for Economic Co-operation and Development, 2007. http://www.pisa.oecd.org/dataoecd/30/17/39703267.pdf .

Radford, Luis, and Luis Puig. "Syntax and Meaning as Sensuous, Visual, Historical Forms of Algebraic Thinking." *Educational Studies in Mathematics* 66 (October 2007): 145–64.

Samuels, Christina. "'Gifted' Label Said to Miss Dynamic Nature of Talent." *Education Week* 8 (October 2008): 1, 18.

Saul, Mark. "Algebra: What Are We Teaching?" In *The Roles of Representation in School Mathematics,* 2001 Yearbook of the National Council of Teachers of Mathematics (NCTM), edited by Albert A. Cuoco, pp. 35–43. Reston, Va.: NCTM, 2001.

Scheaffer, Richard, and Josh Tabor. "Statistics in the High School Mathematics Curriculum—Building Sound Reasoning under Uncertain Conditions." *Mathematics Teacher* 102 (August 2008): 56–61.

Schoenfeld, Alan H. "Beyond the Purely Cognitive: Belief Systems, Social Cognitions, and Metacognitions as Driving Forces in Intellectual Performance." *Cognitive Science* 7 (October–December 1983): 329–63.

Schroeder, Thomas L., and Frank K. Lester, Jr. "Developing Understanding in Mathematics via Problem Solving." In *New Directions for Elementary School Mathematics,* 1989 Yearbook of the National Council of Teachers of Mathematics (NCTM), edited by Paul R. Trafton, pp. 31–56. Reston, Va.: NCTM, 1989.

Secretary's Commission on Achieving Necessary Skills. *What Work Requires of Schools: A SCANS Report for America 2000.* Washington, D.C.: U.S. Department of Labor, 1991. http://wdr.doleta.gov/SCANS/.

Smith, Jack, Beth Herbel-Eisenmann, Amanda Jansen, and Jon Star. "Studying Mathematical Transitions: How Do Students Navigate Fundamental Changes in Curriculum and Pedagogy?" Paper presented at the 2000 annual meeting of the American Educational Research Association, New Orleans, April 2000.

Tapping America's Potential. *Gaining Momentum, Losing Ground.* 2008. http://www.tap2015.org/news/tap_2008_progress.pdf.

Task Force on the Future of American Innovation. *The Knowledge Economy: Is the United States Losing Its Competitive Edge?* Washington, D.C.: Task Force on the Future of American Innovation, 2005.

Tate, William, and Celia Rousseau. "Access and Opportunity: The Political and Social Context of Mathematics Education." In *Handbook of International Research in Mathematics Education,* edited by Lyn D. English, pp. 271–99. Mahwah, N.J.: Lawrence Erlbaum Associates, 2002.

———. "Engineering Change in Mathematics Education." In *Second Handbook of Research on Mathematics Teaching and Learning,* edited by Frank K. Lester, pp. 1206–46. Charlotte, N.C.: Information Age Publishing; Reston, Va.: National Council of Teachers of Mathematics, 2007.

U.S. Census Bureau. *World POPClock Projection.* http://www.census.gov/ipc/ /popclockworld.html.

U.S. Department of Labor. *Number of Jobs Held, Labor Market Activity, and Earnings Growth among the Youngest Baby Boomers: Results from a Longitudinal Study.* Washington, D.C.: U.S. Department of Labor, 2006.

Usiskin, Zalman. "Conceptions of School Algebra and Uses of Variables." In *The Ideas of Algebra, K–12,* 1988 Yearbook of the National Council of Teachers of Mathematics (NCTM), edited by Arthur F. Coxford, pp. 8–19. Reston, Va.: NCTM, 1988.

Walker, Erica N. "Why Aren't More Minorities Taking Advanced Math?" *Educational Leadership* 65 (November 2007): 48–53.

WGBH Educational Foundation. *Learning Math: Data Analysis, Statistics, and Probability.* Video Series. Boston, Mass.: WGBH Educational Foundation, 2001.

Yackel, Erna, and Gila Hanna. "Reasoning and Proof." In *A Research Companion to "Principles and Standards for School Mathematics,"* edited by Jeremy Kilpatrick, W. Gary Martin, and Deborah Shifter, pp. 227–36. Reston, Va.: National Council of Teachers of Mathematics, 2003.

Yerushalmy, Michal, and Beba Shternberg. "Charting a Visual Course to the Concept of Function." In *The Roles of Representation in School Mathematics,* 2001 Yearbook of the National Council of Teachers of Mathematics (NCTM), edited by Albert A. Cuoco, pp. 251–67. Reston, Va.: NCTM, 2001.